CLIMBING HIGHER

Madalene Harris

Here's Life Publishers

P.O. Box 1576, San Bernardino, CA 92402

First printing, March 1989

Published by
HERE'S LIFE PUBLISHERS, INC.
P. O. Box 1576
San Bernardino, CA 92402

Library of Congress Cataloging-in-Publication Data
Harris, Madalene, 1925-
  Climbing higher.

  Includes bibliographies.
  1. Christian life—1960-   . 2. Harris, Madalene, 1925-   . I. Title.
BV4501.2.H3596   1988   248.4   88-30067
ISBN 0-89840-198-4 (pbk.)

Unless otherwise indicated, Scripture quotations are from the *King James Version.*

Scripture quotations designated NIV are from *The Holy Bible, New International Version,* © 1978 by the New York International Bible Society, published by the Zondervan Corporation, Grand Rapids, Michigan.

Scripture quotations designated TLB are from *The Living Bible,* © 1971 by Tyndale House Publishers, Wheaton, Illinois.

Scripture quotations designated NASB are from *The New American Standard Bible,* © The Lockman Foundation 1960, 1962, 1963, 1968, 1971, 1972, 1975, 1977.

For More Information, Write:
L.I.F.E.—P.O. Box A399, Sydney South 2000, Australia
Campus Crusade for Christ of Canada—Box 300, Vancouver, B.C., V6C 2X3, Canada
Campus Crusade for Christ—Pearl Assurance House, 4 Temple Row, Birmingham, B2 5HG, England
Lay Institute for Evangelism—P.O. Box 8786, Auckland 3, New Zealand
Campus Crusade for Christ—P.O. Box 240, Colombo Court Post Office, Singapore 9117
Great Commission Movement of Nigeria—P.O. Box 500, Jos, Plateau State Nigeria, West Africa
Campus Crusade for Christ International—Arrowhead Springs, San Bernardino, CA 92414, U.S.A.

To

*My Wonderful Husband Harlan
and Our Four Precious Children*

*Lenee Schroeder
Harlan Harris, Jr.
Christine Pinello
David Harris*

Appreciation to Those
Who Helped

To Jennifer Hooper who lovingly sacrificed countless hours working through the pages of this manuscript providing valuable insights, corrections, and an objective outlook.

To the the faithful people who committed themselves to pray daily during the writing process:

Muriel and Jack Wienbarg
Yvonne Baker Stock
Judith Rich
Suzanne Lumpkin
Karolee Cason
Bobbie Taylor
June Farr

To Wanda Elliott and the Tuesday Morning Prayer Group for constant support and intercession for the ministry of this book.

To Charette Barta Kvernstoen, highly esteemed friend, for needed encouragement and skillful editing.

To Les Stobbe, President of Here's Life Publishers, whose patience and optimistic expectations gave me the needed strength to persevere.

Contents

The Lure of the Mountains

I love mountains! I've always loved mountains. Born in the Pacific Northwest amidst tall fir trees and in sight of the beautiful Cascade ranges, I am more at home in the high country than the lowlands.

Life, however, seldom regards my preferences. Necessity has demanded that our family live in a variety of places in order to survive economically. One of those places was in the vast plains area of our country where the ground is as flat as my kitchen floor, and nothing grows unless it is planted. Even the few trees coaxed into begrudging existence lean heavily leeward as if to apologize for their scrawny stature and to announce, "I'm not here by choice."

During the several years we lived there, every summer we fled to the Colorado Rocky Mountains for our two-week vacation. It was glorious. We bought a little camping trailer, found an isolated spot near Estes Park and literally walked around with our heads tilted backwards so we wouldn't miss a single breathtaking view.

As our two weeks drew to a close, and I knew we would be heading south to spend another year in the drab flatlands, for at least a day or so I consciously memorized all I saw. The contour of the mountains, the aspen and evergreen landscape, the circular green meadow where herds of elk and big horn sheep grazed, the rushing waters of crystal clear glacial streams tumbling over rocks, and the bluest-of-blue Colorado skies. If I could just etch it all firmly in my memory, then I'd be able to flash it back on the

7

screen of my mind when the low country became more than I could endure.

What a picture of desperation I have just painted! Nevertheless, it describes most Christians I have ever known, myself included for longer than I care to admit. Now and then we get up on the mountain top of spiritual highs, breathing pure air and glimpsing majestic heights, but resolutely we head back down to a predictable lifestyle of spiritual defeat. In short, living a lie and knowing it.

Because of my personal quest to eliminate this chasm between *knowing* and *living,* the energies of my remaining years are dedicated to teaching similar struggling pilgrims what I have learned. Although I cannot say I have fully arrived, I can say in all honesty that I am enjoying more freedom, more overcoming power and more reality in Christ than I ever dreamed possible.

It is one thing to know *who* we are in Christ. The Bible clearly teaches that when we personally receive Jesus Christ as our Savior, we become *new persons.* Simply put, this means that the former person, the old me, no longer sits in the control tower. I need not be subject to the ravages of sin and its accompanying misery.

Learning to live in this dimension presents quite another consideration. *Becoming* that new person doesn't happen overnight. For some Christians, the transformation never occurs. For others, it is a painstakingly slow process. Most of us possess a head full of knowledge coupled to a life devoid of the proof that God's formula actually works out in our day-to-day existence.

The theme *Climbing Higher* alludes to the daily ascent involved in *becoming who I am in Christ.* No one ever reached the top of a peak by wistfully gazing at it and dreaming of someday getting there. It takes a decision, specific equipment and a dogged determination to make it. Reaching the spiritual heights involves much of the same process.

So let's begin our climb.

PART ONE

Knowing Where I Am Going

To begin any journey, a traveler must first determine if he wants to make a trip. Then he must decide where he is going. The world is so full of exciting possibilities that choosing becomes one of the foremost considerations. Even to make a brief trip, such as climbing a nearby mountain, a choice becomes necessary.

CHAPTER 1

Yes, But Suffer Me First...

". . . Never allow plans to be so 'scheduled'
that you find it difficult to respond
to the Spirit's working."[1]

The whole world stands in awe of Olympic champions. During Florence Griffith Joyner's gold medal performances in Seoul, South Korea, everyone ran to their TV sets and watched admiringly.

But what makes an Olympic winner? To find out, I interviewed one of the visiting psychologists at the United States Olympic Training Center in Colorado Springs.

According to Dr. Jim Davis, champions set goals that are concrete and specific. Then they clearly visualize the attaining of those goals.[2]

A goal such as "being the best athlete I can," or "I want to please my parents," is not a winning attitude. Dr. Davis pointed out that "only those athletes who specifically state in precise terms their objective tend to create a clear enough mental image to sustain prolonged pursuit."

When applied to the developing of spiritual champions, the analogy is equally apt. Most of us are trying just to be the best Christian possible, whatever that is. It's like shooting a .22 caliber rifle into the sky and hoping a bullet magically hits the target. Or the way we customarily pray for foreign missionaries—"God bless all the missionaries wherever they are." Such effort which aims at nothing in particular will surely hit the same.

Let's Get Specific

Because generalized endeavor always tends toward mediocrity, throughout this study we will deal with specific, concrete principles designed to enable all believers to achieve God's ultimate purpose for their lives.

Let me be candid. This book is not for the spiritual dabbler, the one who seeks instant cures or "quick fixes." Such phenomena may exist in the medical world, but not spiritually.

Neither is it for the religious "flitter." You know the type—frantically running around to conferences, retreats, meetings and the like, hoping to be spoon-fed at the hands of self-styled experts rather than to face the truth and grow up in Christ.

Frankly, the overcoming life God clearly offers in His Word comes only to the believer who is determined to seize it at any cost. He/she has reached a point where nothing else can satisfy. The will is set, the mind is determined and the course, however painful, is embraced.

Probably the first (and most difficult) hurdle involves the determining of priorities. Desire may be strong to become all God wants us to become. But we soon discover the distressing fact that *desire is not ability*. If we are ever to become who we are in Christ, our lives must be rearranged so that we have time to pursue the qualities designed to produce that life.

Comparing again the Christian winner to the Olympic champion, the obvious fact cannot be ignored that trainees must make winning the top priority of their lives. If days are crowded with lesser objectives, even worthwhile pursuits, there is never time to get at the most important goal: becoming the person we were divinely designed to be.

The "I'll Do It Someday" Syndrome

The magnificent capitol building in Salem, Oregon, burned to the ground on April 25, 1935. My husband's aunt and uncle, residents of that city most of their lives, remember the incident clearly. Perhaps too clearly for their own emotional comfort.

On that fateful day, they received a call that Uncle Roy's only brother had suffered a serious injury. A broken limb from a falling tree had penetrated his abdomen, infection had set in, and he had been rushed to the Stayton Hospital in critical condition. Stopping at a restaurant to eat before a possible long vigil at the hospital, Uncle Roy and Aunt Beulah noticed a small column of smoke no larger than a finger rising from the dome of the capitol building.

"Look at that smoke," Aunt Beulah said.

"Wonder where it's coming from?" Uncle Roy responded.

"Looks like it's near the state house. Do you think we should call the fire department?"

"Oh, I don't know," Uncle Roy said. "They probably have it under control by now."

"Well, that's true," Aunt Beulah agreed. "Besides, it's important that we get to the hospital as soon as we can."

"Why don't we call when we get there?" Uncle Roy concluded. "Then if it's anything important, they can still do something about it."

With the stress of the brother's emergency, they forgot. The day passed quickly, and soon it was time to head home.

Coming back from Stayton near to midnight, they took a short cut. At the top of the hill they saw a mush of flame and acrid haze permeating the air. With a jolt they remembered their earlier resolve.

"Oh, Roy!" cried Aunt Beulah. "You don't think—surely not the state house? Oh, no! It just can't be!"

But it was. They drove straight to her parents, quickly woke them up and took them out to see the saddest and most spectacular fire of their lives. They stayed long enough to see the beautiful building collapse. Unbelief mingled with remorse — they really had meant to make that call. If only they had suspected the critical nature of what they saw earlier in the day. If only they had known.

It's a Matter of Choice

Procrastination can be a thief which robs us of precious opportunities. And when our priorities are confused, procrastination becomes a way of life. Each of us is constantly faced with choices, large and small. As soon as we awaken in the morning, choices begin. Shall I get out of bed early and get going? Or shall I take just a few more minutes? From that first decision and throughout the day, our lives consist of a multitude of choices.

Just such an insignificant matter as getting out of bed early one morning changed the entire course of our lives. Little did we dream so much hung upon so little.

It all happened in Washington D.C. a few months after my husband and I were married. Many of the churches in the D.C. area were engaged in a simultaneous evangelism effort, and ours was one of them. My husband was the assistant to an elderly pastor who didn't want to turn loose of the control of anything. We knew we wouldn't stay long in this unchallenging situation.

A city-wide breakfast was scheduled for 6 A.M. Monday morning for all the pastors, evangelists, and church staff workers. My husband planned to attend. Until, that is, the alarm rang at 5 o'clock that morning. He wearily rolled over and shut off the noisy intruder.

"I don't think I'll go after all," he said. Immediately he turned and fell back asleep.

The longer I thought about it, the more I knew he must go, and so I woke him again. "You really should go."

"But I don't want to."

Finally I insisted. "Harlan, I feel very strongly that you should get up and go."

He did. It was a cold, gray, snowy January morning, and Harlan discovered when he arrived that a number of wives had failed to insist that their husbands get out of bed. Attendance was sparse.

Even the designated song director didn't make it, and Harlan was asked to lead the singing. Little did he suspect that one of the evangelists, a pastor of a huge southern congregation, was looking for an assistant. The moment my husband stood up to direct the music, the pastor knew he had found his man. By the time breakfast was over, arrangements were made to fly us both to North Carolina.

The rest is history. The pastor resigned soon after we moved, and my husband stepped into his pulpit to remain seven years. Those were among the happiest years of our lives.

Decision making is not easy. Women especially find themselves pulled in many directions, torn as to what God really wants of them. Numbers of incidents in my life have shattered me because I really didn't know what I was supposed to choose from among several conflicting claims. Should I go with my husband? Or would it be better to support my child by attending his school function? Or should I stay home and perform necessary domestic duties? Or what about that important meeting at church?

Almost every child of God desires to follow Jesus Christ. However poor the performance, the desire is there. Often strongly so. What then creates so astonishing a difference between desire and ability?

Desire Is Not Enough

An incident in the life of Jesus clearly illustrates the answer. As He was speaking to a great crowd, a man came to Him declaring, "Lord, I'll follow you wherever you go."[3] Obviously he possessed a great desire to follow Jesus.

But when Jesus said, "Foxes have holes, and birds of the air have nests, but the Son of Man has no place to lay His head,"[4] this would-be follower decided such a life might be pretty tough. We hear nothing more of him.

Immediately afterward Jesus called to another, "Follow me."

"Lord, I will follow you," came the prompt reply, "but first let me . . ."[5]

There is our dilemma. We really want to follow Jesus. We really mean to do it some day. But at the moment too many other things are pressing in on us, so we push it to the back of our minds thinking we have plenty of time.

Multi-talented people are the worst, I think. Being adept at many things may not be an asset because it is nearly impossible to focus on one major goal long enough to excel. Dabbling in a different pursuit daily may lead to a varied and exciting life, but one of unbearable mediocrity as well.

The disillusionment of a life so spent doesn't register during youth. It is during those later years when the "it-might-have-been-so-different" regrets haunt one.

Our Greatest Enemy

An overcommitted, unfocused life is a sure route to spiritual disaster. Reasons vary as to why so many Christians overextend themselves. Often the inner child still struggles to please a demanding parent. For others, basic insecurity is the culprit, convincing us that a busy schedule automatically lends status. The inability to say a firm no plagues the individual with a poor self-image.

The truth is, our "flesh" loves to be busy. Inner restlessness drives us on, and our minds register guilt if we slow down the least bit. Therefore, we never find time to do the things that really count.

One writer calls it hurry sickness. "It comes from our urge to live and do everything in a hurry. As a consequence, we are living at a pace too fast for our bodies."[6]

Every grueling day becomes a race against the clock simply to beat deadlines. Tasks that aren't screaming for attention can safely be set aside for a more convenient season. It doesn't matter how important they are. If they can wait, that's exactly what happens. Often forever.

I meet such people all the time who bemoan the irreversible reality that opportunity has passed them by. They will never again be able to accomplish the things they've dreamed about for a lifetime. "Where have the years flown?" they ask. "Why didn't I take advantage of those opportunities when I could?"

Time Plays Tricks on Us

For several years my husband and I worked with teenagers in North Carolina. Every summer we boarded from fifty to one hundred of those energetic youth into Greyhound buses and headed for a Colorado Young Life Ranch via Chicago. Since we both had attended college near Chicago and knew the area well, this side trip provided a bit of excitement for those small-town kids.

One of the main attractions for them was "Skid Row" down on West Madison and South State streets. We wanted them to see the awful retribution hounding those who make hurtful choices in life. Those kids had never seen destitute winos staggering about, or bums sleeping in doorways and parks, or flamboyant street solicitors. Beggars shuffled among passers-by with outstretched hand.

We stopped once to talk to a tattered, unshaven man who appeared halfway sober. My husband told him he wanted his youthful group to see the results of wrong choices. Promptly, the man said he was a former college professor who had been an alcoholic and lost all ability to lead a normal life. His family left him, his job disintegrated, and he became penniless. Skid Row seemed to be his only option.

"Kids, let me tell you," he began slowly. "Don't run the risk of becoming like me. Stay away from the bottle. Do what this man tells you to do, otherwise you may end up in this same kind of living hell."

He turned to walk away. Suddenly he cast a wistful glance over his shoulder and muttered, "Time has played tricks on me."

Knowing Where I Am Going

The truth is, time plays tricks on all of us unless we make a firm choice and set our wills as to the direction we are heading. In other words, we must declare our destination. And the sooner, the better.

I need to ask myself as a woman: Will I be a Martha, always busy about "many things"? Or will I be a Mary, making the wiser choice to sit at the feet of Jesus? "Mary has chosen what is better," Jesus said, "and it will not be taken away from her."[7]

Much controversy surrounds the "Mary/Martha Syndrome." Wherever I travel, women say to me, "I really want to be a Mary, but my circumstances force me into the Martha role." Who doesn't understand that? And yet, if we are not careful, we camouflage the truth behind such a logical sounding excuse. The fact is, we would all rather stay inordinately busy in this accomplishment-oriented world than simply sit at the feet of Jesus.

I believe the Lord's answer indicates that Martha was fussing over unnecessary details. As women, most of us know what He meant. It satisfies a certain sense of pride to prepare lavish company meals when a simple supper would suffice. We are worn out and cranky at everyone after working so many hours. Needless hours.

The most difficult balance to achieve in today's society involves the working woman. With more than half of the women in America daily leaving their homes for the workplace, and a large percentage of them juggling a career and the rearing of children alone, it is understandable that spare moments are at a premium. But for the heart that "follows hard" after Jesus, time will be found to sit at His feet. It may be during lunch hour—preparing an extra sack lunch in the morning and finding a quiet spot to be with the Lord while colleagues maintain a social hour. Or it may be to sacrifice a bit of morning sleep to get up early and meet the Lord. Whatever it takes, it's worth the trouble.

Mary's heart was focused upon the Lord, while her sister's was distracted by the cares of this life. "It must be God first, God second, and God third until the life is faced steadily with God, and no one else is of any account whatever," Oswald Chambers wrote.[8] And here is the secret. If our hearts are focused upon the Lord, even the cares of this life will not distract us. We will accomplish necessary duty in His strength, not ours. But that duty will not crowd out what is most important if we have predetermined our ultimate goal.

Crucial Questions

What do you really want from life? As a Christian, is it enough simply to be driven from one urgency to another, finally reaching the end of your days exhausted and realizing you haven't accomplished God's design for you?

Where are you in the river of life? Lloyd Ogilvie asks, "Are you swimming against the current of the Lord's plan or flowing with it? He wants to do more than just keep us afloat while we resist the flow."[9]

Is it even possible to take control of a life after wasting years in secondary pursuits? Can anyone get a fresh start and head in a different direction?

I hear people saying, "Nobody ever changes. We are what we are, and we're always going to be that way." Often these are well-meaning people, Christians who profess to sincerely believe this.

Without hesitation I say to them, "If I agreed with you, I would never write another line or publicly speak another word as long as I live." If Christians, in whom the living Christ dwells, cannot change, then we had better trash the Bible. And the Holy Spirit, too.

So the first step, even before examining priorities,

might be to settle the issue of whether it is possible to change.

- Does the Bible say, "I can do all things through Christ Who strengthens me,"[10] or doesn't it?
- Does that mean you?
- Does "all" mean all things God calls you to do, or just a selected few things?
- Does "through Christ" really mean that you don't have to depend upon your own limited abilities, but that you have access to His unlimited resources to effect change in your life?

Don't be defeated by a feeling of hopelessness. Christians really can change. But it never happens by our own limited abilities. Only Jesus Christ's power operating within can produce necessary change.

So let's begin with the exhilarating possibility that yes, we can change because of our new nature. That's the nature we received when we personally invited Jesus Christ to be our Savior. The Bible clearly says that we are "a new creation in Christ Jesus."[11]

All we have to do is exercise a small amount of faith to believe we are new creations in Christ Jesus. From that moment it is possible to begin moving in a totally different direction than ever before.

What's Next?

We'll never progress until we examine our priorities. What we do with our time largely determines the direction of our lives. If you are feeling pressed, always behind, never able to find time for anything you really want to do, you already know you're in trouble. It won't get better unless you take matters into your own hands.

It will be helpful if you make a list of everything you do. Omit nothing. Beside each entry, indicate the amount of time you spend each week at that particular thing, and then use the following code:

> E — Essential.
> N — Non-essential, but something I like to do.
> D — Dispensible — just takes up time.
> S — Simply excess — wish I didn't have to do this.

Pray about each entry after making your list. Ask God for wisdom to show you clearly what His will is for your life. God says, "If any of you lack wisdom, let him ask of God . . ."[12] Before taking the next step, wait to receive a definite word from God.

Unclutter. Get rid of the time wasters. No matter what — telephone calls, personal appointments, letters, upsetting people — eliminate from your life activities God reveals as excess baggage.

Memorize this statement: "Oh, I'd love to do it, (dramatic pause) but I can't." No further explanation. These nine little words, when applied consistently, will save an enormous amount of time and emotional duress. We trap ourselves into commitments we loathe simply because we are afraid we might offend someone.

Be tough. Make up your mind that for the rest of your life, you will be in charge of your hours and days instead of allowing people to push their self-centered demands upon you. Stay in control. Then give your life to God in a new way.

> *The clock of life is wound but once*
> *And no one has the power*
> *To say just when the hands will stop,*
> *At late, or early hour.*
> *Now is the only time we own*
> *To do God's precious will.*
> *Don't wait until tomorrow,*
> *For the clock may then be still.*[13]

CHAPTER 2

What If?

*"All our fears are wicked,
and we fear because
we will not nourish ourselves in faith."*[1]

It was 11:30 P.M., September 21, 1986, at London's Sheraton Skyline Hotel. We had just fallen asleep when the telephone rang. I fumbled for the lamp switch and picked up the receiver.

"Did you and Harlan hear the news tonight?" our team coordinator's tense voice inquired.

"No, what was it?"

"A terrorist group has threatened to blow up an American plane this week. I haven't told anyone else in the group, but I want you and Harlan to be praying about it."

"Oh—yes—of course. We'll do it. Thanks, Mike. Thanks a lot."

Thoughts of sleep vanished as I told the news to my husband. Cold fingers of fear clasped my heart.

"Let's get out of bed right now and pray about it," Harlan said at last. When we climbed back, I wondered if sleep would come again. For a long time I lay awake. The rest of our American group would be flying out of London's Heathrow Airport in the morning, but we had scheduled an extra week of sightseeing on British Rail trains. We would not be leaving the country until early next week.

I prayed again for our friends' safety. Then, I carefully counted the days. If the terrorists meant what they said, Harlan and I would probably be safe. What if we weren't, though? What if they planted their bomb in our plane?

I knew I was ready to die. My eternal destination had been settled years earlier when I received Jesus Christ as personal Savior. Why was I anxious then? Besides, the airport bombings two weeks ago had been in Paris. So continental Europe would be the most likely target—not England. With that I committed the situation to the Lord and fell asleep.

When we knew our friends had flown home safely, not another thought of the threat entered my mind during our busy week of sightseeing throughout England, Scotland, and Wales. Not, that is, until the day before we were scheduled to fly out of London on Pan Am.

Riding the train from Cardiff, Wales, toward Portsmouth, England, we spotted a discarded newspaper. We were hungry for American news, so we grabbed it before anyone else noticed and glanced at the headlines:

TERRORIST BOMB THREAT
IN LONDON'S HEATHROW

So now it was pinpointed to the precise area we would be departing from in the morning. The "what if's" began again.

I knew I had a clear choice. I could live either by faith or by fear. The decision was mine. Sitting on that train, I wrestled with my choice, realizing there is no middle ground between faith and fear. It is one or the other.

The Development of Anxiety

Every issue we face carries the same decision. In this accelerated society, internal anxiety is such an accepted way of life that few of us even stop to question whether its existence is necessary. We are scarcely aware that this subtle companion drains off precious vitality and prevents us from accomplishing our most cherished goals.

Anxiety slips in so unobtrusively that we are not even aware of its existence until suddenly—wham! We're a total wreck, and we wonder what wiped us out.

Perhaps a good definition of anxiety is inner apprehension or fear in the absence of actual danger.[2] Anxiety naturally accompanies real danger. That is a normal reaction. We are not considering this type of anxiety or fear. Our primary focus is the constant apprehension most of us carry around day and night for which we can find no specific cause.

Most often it begins in childhood. Parents who are inwardly secure surround their children with a stable atmosphere and produce secure children. But such parents are few and far between. Usually they become more secure after the children are grown, and the tensions are relaxed, and the noise subsides. It is only then that they have time to reflect upon whether they want to continue this madness or do something about it. It's too late for the kids, though.

But it need not be so. The constant state of inner anxiety can be recognized and overcome early in life.

Tracing the evolution of fear might follow a course similar to this:

1. An event occurs. Anxiety over an unmanageable situation develops. We may have experienced failure, humiliation, or punishment.

2. We firmly resolve to avoid the pain of a similar circumstance in the future.

3. Fear of experiencing the same emotion develops.

4. In the effort to avoid such situations in the future, anxiety slips into other areas of our conscious and subconscious minds.

5. Ultimately we become inwardly anxious most of the time, always expecting the worst to happen.

A Typical Example

My mother died when I was eight years old. I knew

she had cancer. Though no one told me directly, I had over-
heard the term.

From before my birth, my parents had been
engrossed in a religious system which taught there is no
life, truth nor intelligence in sin, sickness or death. In other
words, we did not believe in sin, sickness or death. I was
carefully schooled in this philosophy.

So, of course, we couldn't speak about sickness. And
we didn't believe in death, so no one could prepare me for
this death of the most important person in my whole world.
When it happened, I couldn't be told that my mother died.
The explanation was simply, "She has fallen asleep."

But she didn't wake up. In my childish eight-year-
old mind I suspected what had happened. Yet I never could
be sure she actually died because no one would tell me. And
cancer must have been the culprit, I reasoned — whatever
cancer was.

From that time until adulthood when Jesus Christ
delivered me from the fear of cancer and death, I harbored
an inordinate dread of both. I really didn't know why, because I had buried my grief so deeply that it never surfaced
to my conscious mind. I simply avoided funerals, cancer
patients, and any conversation or literature regarding
either. A great portion of my energies became devoted to
this scheme of escape.

If you think such avoidance was a simple matter,
add to it the complication that my husband was a pastor of
large congregations. Undoubtedly I was considered heart-
less by a great many parishioners. No one (not even I) knew
why I could not face these two formidable enemies, however
commonplace they were in my world. Many cancer patients
needed my encouragement, but when I looked at them, all
I saw was death. So I wouldn't look.

To say that anxiety was confined to these two areas
would be far from the truth. Gradually I became so inwardly anxious all the time that my every waking moment
became a scramble to drown out tension.

Then one day a biopsy declared my husband ill with cancer. I had to either face this dread thing or fall apart. I fell apart for a while. Finally the realization hit me that my husband had no one to lean upon during this life-and-death struggle except me. At that point I began to deal with reality.

It was a slow process. At first I faked it for his sake. Eventually the deep, hidden metamorphosis gradually churned up the lifelong dread that began when I was eight. At length I was able to come to terms with it.

How Prevalent Is Anxiety?

It's probably a good idea at this point to examine fear and anxiety in our own particular experience. Cecil Osborne points out that psychologists agree in general that "every action is an effort to avoid anxiety."[3] What an amazing statement. Its all-inclusiveness forces us to consider the implications in our own lives.

Another writer indicates that many people organize their lives around the effort to avoid anxiety so that "the fear of fear consumes their waking hours and anxiety about anxiety brings such tension and stress that it becomes self-fulfilling."[4] This may explain the patchwork of senseless pursuits we engage ourselves in without knowing why.

If we could honestly examine our true motives for the choices we make each day, we might be startled to discover the fear that underlies most of them. How many activities, for instance, do we embrace simply because we are afraid of what someone might think if we didn't?

On the other hand, how many things do we avoid simply to decrease the pain of anxiety (things God may desire to use for our growth and development)?

Even the most anxiety-prone believer can become a calm, secure person. You will note that I said believer. Apart from Jesus Christ's life within, there is little possibility of change. The dog-eat-dog world in which we live produces nothing but fear and anxiety. Even the most hardened criminal will admit, particularly after receiving Jesus Christ as Savior, that fear consumed him like a voracious malignancy.

Fear does that same thing to everyone. It saps our energies and consumes precious creative powers God intends to use for His glory.

Can God Help Us?

"Come to me, all you who are weary and burdened, and I will give you rest . . ."[5]

The Bible is crammed with promises of inner peace to the child of God. When you get into the habit of focusing on a specific promise from God, claiming it, and standing upon it no matter how you feel or don't feel, anxiety flees.

One of the Scripture passages I puzzled over for years said, "There remains a rest to the people of God. For he that is entered into His rest has ceased from his own works . . . let us labor therefore to enter into that rest . . ."[6]

I understood this "rest" to be an inner condition, and the way to attain it was to stop striving in my own strength to get through the struggles of each day and instead begin taking God's strength. In other words, stop living in the realm of self-effort and begin walking in the Spirit of God.

It was the next phrase that caused my dilemma — *let us labor to enter that rest.* Labor and rest are not compatible. Just as soon as I began laboring to eliminate self-effort, I found myself inwardly tense. This can't be it, I thought.

As time passed and I prayed earnestly for inner peace, now and then I caught glimpses of the truth. I would enjoy brief periods of God's "peace that passes understanding." Afterwards, examining the process, I recognized a little pattern:

● Things had gotten out of hand, and I knew I had nowhere to turn except to God.

- In great distress of soul I gave it all to Him, relinquishing my ability to solve the unsolvable.

- I claimed a promise, like "My God shall supply all your need . . ."[7] and by sheer faith believed God would come through.

- Immediately God's peace flooded my inner being like sunshine after a storm, and when the solution came, it was just like God promised: ". . . exceeding abundantly above all that I could ask or think . . ."[8]

Gradually the contradiction between rest and labor became reconciled. The more I repeated the process, the less anxiety I experienced. And, paradoxical as it may sound, it became actual labor to enter into that rest. Eventually I didn't wait until my circumstances were so out-of-hand that I was desperate. If the slightest anxiety surfaced, I went through the formula until it became automatic.

Paul admonishes, "Do not be anxious about anything."[9] To test my anxiety level, I ask myself the question: "Now, let's see—am I anxious about this thing? Is there even the *slightest* anxiety about it?"

If there is, then I am in disobedience because I am clearly commanded not to be anxious about anything. Many Christians feel they shouldn't bother God with trivialities. God's Word doesn't substantiate that outlook. "Not anything" means exactly that—*nothing!*

How Can I Overcome Anxiety?

Although it takes time to completely eradicate the anxious syndrome, it can be done. Here are some practical steps to transform our thinking and allow Jesus Christ to take full control of our emotions so that they are available to be used for God's glory.

1. It is important to *recognize the source of fear.* "God has not given us the spirit of fear," the Bible says in 2 Timothy 1:7. Only two power sources control this universe, God and Satan, so it doesn't take a mathe-

matician to determine the origin of fear. Memorize that verse, and the moment fear grips your heart, quote it out loud.

2. *Do not rationalize.* Often we think fear is a natural response to circumstances out of our control. If God says the spirit of fear is not from Him, then make no mistake—all fear is rooted in Satan's domain. Stand your ground. Don't believe the lie.

3. *Ask God to reveal hidden sources of fear.* This step may be the most difficult, because more than likely painful childhood memories will be dredged up. In the process, memories which have been buried for years must be relived. Keep in mind that healing from these memories cannot occur unless you know what they are. Not only is fear of cancer and death gone from me, but the pain of losing my mother has been resolved as well. God is faithful. If you ask, you will receive.

4. *Take strong measures to rout this destroyer.* If Satan is the source of fear, then deal directly with him. This may sound "off-the-wall," but I assure you it works. Just as I speak to God, I also speak to Satan. I quote God's Word to him. I remind him that he has no power over me because Jesus Christ stripped him of any power or authority at the cross. I audibly rebuke him and bind his grip on me. God says, "Resist the devil and he will flee from you."[10] That's exactly what he does. Instantly.

It may be necessary to repeat this procedure again and again until fear is completely gone, but I give Satan absolutely no room to operate within my life.

5. *Boldly face the thing you fear.* Not in your own strength, but God's. Arm yourself with His promises, and then go forth.

In my case, it became necessary to visibly confront cancer. Since I was eight years old I had hardly spoken the word or consciously thought of it. Now that suddenly my husband was battling it, cancer became a household familiarity. At the clinic where my husband was being treated, I forced myself to talk to cancer patients.

More than a decade has passed since my husband's biopsy. Not only have I overcome my mortal fear of cancer and death, but now I go out of my way to visit cancer victims and try to give them hope and encouragement. Many of them have told me, "You're the only person in the world who has given me the hope that I may live in spite of my condition." Numbers of these people have recovered just as my husband has.

6. *Help others overcome their fears.* Often I do this in a joking way at first. When someone says to me, "I'm scared of such-and such," I laugh and tell them, "God has not given you the spirit of scared, you know." Usually this is the beginning of an earnest conversation about how they can be delivered from fear.

Whenever I help others, I receive the joy of seeing them set free to become what God has created them to become. My young friend, Mary Ann, is a good example.

Mary Ann's husband is Jewish. He grew up in an Israeli kibbutz. Soon after their first grandson was born, Saul's parents offered to send airplane tickets to this young couple so they could see Daniel.

"I just can't go to Israel," Mary Ann told me. "I am scared to go."

I used my stock answer. "God has not given you the spirit of scared, Mary Ann."

"I know," she smiled.

Then I asked her, "Why are you so scared, Mary Ann? It's a wonderful place, and I'd go again in a minute."

"Well, if you must know, I am deathly afraid of airplanes."

"Don't you know that traveling by air is safer than by car?"

"Maybe," she replied. "But my mother is just the same. She still won't travel by plane."

Having identified the exact fear and its origin, we then began a series of in-depth conversations about fear in the life of a believer. Mary Ann and Saul finally made the trip. As a result, the whole direction of their lives has changed as Saul is realizing a strong call from God to eventually return to his beloved Israel and evangelize his people.

Additionally, when Mary Ann faced and overcame this enormous hurdle, she recognized how much of her life was governed by anxiety. Having triumphed in one area, she moved to others and is learning to live in the peace God has promised.

Everything Changes

It's a wonderful world out there when we live in the absence of fear and anxiety. To wake up each morning in a state of eager anticipation instead of dull dread is like returning to childhood and walking starry-eyed into a toy store at Christmas. It is worth every effort needed to rout this thief of God's promised possessions.

Don't be distressed if you have lived so long in this miserable state. Even if you have only a few years left, they could be more productive for the kingdom of God than all the rest combined.

I view my own life in that perspective. Winning over anxiety came to me after I had been a Christian nearly thirty years. I cannot go back and relive those years, but the opportunity I now have to become the person God created me to be more than compensates for the loss.

> *All the water in the world*
> *However hard it tried,*
> *Could never, never sink a ship*
> *Unless it got inside.*
> *All the hardships of this world,*
> *Might wear you pretty thin,*
> *But they won't hurt you one least bit,*
> *Unless you take them in.*[11]

CHAPTER 3

Lord, Why?

*". . . the greatest reason for a complaining spirit
is lack of contentment . . .
Because we are not content,
we become contentious."*[1]

Some of the happiest people on earth have problems enough to stagger the imagination. Yet they never complain.

On the other hand, chronic complainers make themselves and everyone around them miserable. Often they have little cause for unhappiness; still they find plenty of opportunity to complain. Sometimes I want to shake them and say, "Stop! If you keep on, God may give you good reason to continue!"

A lady I once knew in our church was a typical example of the chronic complainer. Actually, she was one of the most thoughtful, giving persons in the church, but whenever I saw her or she called on the telephone, I was forced to listen to a long list of ailments. It seemed impossible that so many things could go wrong in one person's life.

Chronic complainers seldom understand that the disgruntled words they send out can ricochet right back to their own doorstep. A vivid example a few years ago was the air controllers strike which President Reagan allowed to backfire. These men threatened to walk off their jobs and paralyze not only the airline industry, but the entire nation as well.

What was their reasoning? Although many of them were earning more than $50,000 a year, they complained that their salaries were not enough to compensate for the emotional stress they were subjected to day after day.

No one denied those pressures existed. But the struggle for survival among airline companies with many being forced into bankruptcy swept the tide of public sentiment against the air controllers. This was not a time for one segment of the industry to demand excessive increases in salary. If anything, cutbacks were in order.

When labor union negotiations failed and the air controllers' demands were not met, President Reagan warned that he would allow these strikers to lose their jobs if they did not return voluntarily. Still they wouldn't back down. The President acted, the controllers were fired, others hired, and to this day the complainers have not regained their former jobs or recouped their losses.

One can't help but wonder how many of the former controllers regret not yielding before the ax fell. Editorial observers have since noted that as a result of the aborted air controllers strike, our nation hasn't been troubled with many others. It was a costly lesson, but usually they are. Preventative measures are far more palatable than consequences.

Complaining Is Habit-forming

Complaining reminds me of overeating. If I allow myself for one day to eat unrestrainedly, I am hungrier the next day. If I continue to indulge my unruly appetite, soon it catapults to uncontrolled proportions until eating becomes a compulsion. All day long the thought of food gnaws at my subconscious. And I don't have to spell out what eventually happens. The numbers on my scale move out of control.

A similar process evolves if we do not recognize and curb this spirit of complaining. The more we do it, the easier it becomes. An inner attitude of discontent with every person and circumstance sets in, and we find ourselves grumbling our dissatisfied way through life. The end result is an all-consuming negative outlook.

"Oh, I'm just a realist," complainers say. One man justified his negative outlook by insisting that if he always expects the worst and it doesn't happen, he is never disappointed.

"That sounds logical," I told him. "But why are you such a miserable person if your formula is so great?"

"Well, I'm not actually unhappy. I just don't find many things to get excited about."

It's a Contagious Disease, Too

I have noted a strange tendency in myself. Although usually I am a happy, positive person, I change when I get around chronic complainers. Before I realize what is happening, I find myself playing their game. It becomes a "can you top this?" contest. Or, I take the opposite course and retreat into silence until I can get away from them, secretly vowing to avoid contact in the future.

A poster in a nursing home once attracted my attention. It said:

"The only thing more contagious than optimism
is pessimism."

At the time I read the statement, I thought such advice was especially needed for older people. The longer I ponder its truth, the more I realize how desperately all of us require this constant reminder.

Let's take a quick look at the negative effects of being a complainer:

● A complaining spirit begets a joyless attitude. After a while nothing looks good.

● The more we complain, the more negative we become in our overall outlook.

- A negative outlook leads to inner doubts and a general dissatisfaction with all of life.
- Often a critical spirit develops.
- People tend to avoid us, and we become lonely.
- Much illness is due to a negative outlook. Complaining about symptoms magnifies them in our minds and intensifies suffering.
- Worst of all, a complaining spirit is grounded in unbelief and blocks spiritual growth and inner vitality.

Are Some People Born Complainers?

A negative, complaining spirit, like anxiety, is a learned process. Our best teachers are our earliest ones— parents or other family members. We did not choose the circumstances into which we were born, and we cannot change the past. But we can change the present and diminish those early influences that shaped us before we gave consent.

Isn't it strange that God so seldom puts people of similar disposition together in a marriage? My own is no exception.

Because my parents, especially my father, provided excellent role models by displaying a cheerful, optimistic spirit no matter what the circumstances, I tend to have a similar disposition.

No one suffered more setbacks than my father. His youthful wife died, leaving him alone with three small children. Our home burned soon thereafter. Housekeeper after housekeeper alternately abused his children or stole every valuable object in the home. His only son was killed at age twenty.

But he always looked for the rainbow. He was the happiest, most content person in the world despite continual hardship. As a result, both my sister and I emerged with the same indomitable outlook.

Conversely, my husband grew up in a family of complainers. Although his parents became Christians earlier than mine, the home atmosphere did not appreciably change. Consequently, my husband has been battling a negative attitude for years. But because I have seen him change drastically, I know it can be done despite one's early home influences.

The Hidden Agenda Behind Complaining

Whether we admit it or not, unbelief and disobedience are the underlying reasons for a complaining spirit.

God's Word is clear: "Do everything without complaining or arguing."[2] This is a command, not an option. He doesn't qualify the statement and excuse us if things suddenly go wrong and it's not our fault. He says *everything*—and I take that to be all-inclusive. He is talking about every single circumstance whether desirable or not. When I complain, I am in essence saying, "I really don't believe God has arranged these circumstances or that He could change them if He desired." If I did believe it, I wouldn't need to complain. I'd know my only safety is in the center of His will no matter what happens.

The same God who told me not to complain also said, "In everything give thanks, for this is the will of God in Christ Jesus concerning you."[3] How is it possible to give thanks and complain at the same time?

Is it hypocritical to say I'm thankful for my problems when I don't feel thankful? Not really, because God assures us that ". . . all things work together for good . . ."[4] Even when it looks disastrous, I can be certain that these self-same predicaments will be miraculously transformed under the skilled knife of the divine surgeon. He might do a little hurtful cutting on me through the process, but it will only be for my good.

Can We Change Lifelong Patterns?

During early adolescence and a very impressionable

stage of my development, I was permanently influenced by a quotation carved in concrete. Above the large triple-door entrance to my high school was engraved:

> "You are now becoming
> what you are about to be."

At first I didn't understand the meaning. But day after day as I walked under those words, it dawned on me that whoever I hoped to be someday, I was becoming that person every minute I spent inside the school building.

Many years have passed, but the truth of those words has not changed. Whatever I am today is the cumulative result of all that has gone on before in my life—my circumstances, my choices, my decisions, my words, my actions. And whatever I become in future years is dependent upon the decisions I am presently making.

If you don't like the person you are, or if your life is moving in an undesirable direction, it is never too late to make a change. Even though I have crossed over the halfway mark of life, I continue to evaluate myself before God on a regular basis and make needful alterations.

Change never happens unless we face ourselves with brutal honesty. The longer we delay this procedure of self-disclosure, the more set-in-concrete our responses become. A few probing questions related to positive/negative reactions will serve to pinpoint where we are in this particular aspect of the becoming process:

- Am I generally more negative than positive in my responses?
- Do I avoid admitting my bad outlook by insisting that I am a realist, and that other people live in a fantasy world?
- Do I rationalize my attitude by labeling positive people as "out of touch with reality," thereby making myself more comfortable?
- Where would I place myself as to the degree of com-

plaining I indulge in daily: Never? Seldom? Only When Warranted? Often? Excessive?

● In which of the above categories would the members of my family place me? (To be objective, why not ask them?)

It may be necessary to critically evaluate dialogue patterns in order to get an accurate reading. Listen carefully to what you say. We all tend to be defensive rather than totally honest when it comes to admitting weakness.

Even though I am basically a person who complains little, I still fall unaware into the complainer's trap at times. Living in a negative world rubs off on the strongest of us. When I catch myself in a complaining frame of mind, I find it helpful to take a large writing pad and rule a line down the center to make two columns. I label these columns as follows:

What I acutally said:	What I could have said:
I am sick of this stove. We need a new one.	*Harlan, could you fix this burner so it will burn properly?*
I just hate these cloudy days. I never feel like doing anything when the weather is bad.	*This is not my favorite kind of weather, but I'm going to have a great day anyway.*

The above are merely two examples of actual statements I made this past week. Fill in your own so you can begin to work toward a more positive outlook.

What You Say Is What You Get

I do not profess to understand this principle, but I do know from long years of observation that what we speak, either negatively or positively, molds our innermost attitude. Even further, it influences the attitudes and behavior of those around us.

To prove my theory, I have experimented extensively with varying sizes of groups from small clusters of two to five persons in perhaps a luncheon setting, or larger gatherings. When I note a negative, complaining, or judgmental spirit predominating, I quietly begin counteracting the prevailing mood by carefully placed statements.

When someone is complaining in a small group, I suggest a possible benefit as a direct result of the unpleasant circumstance. Or if I am hearing criticism, I try to remember an admirable quality of the victim and mention it in an offhanded way. I am often surprised how a single statement can change the whole tone of a conversation.

The same process affects larger groups. Positive, optimistic declarations reverse the emotional climate. A great deal of satisfaction can be realized by leaving a previously unhappy group of people smiling instead of grumbling.

Complaining Precipitates Illnesses

Probably the worst side-effect of a complaining attitude is the eventual amplification of physical ailments. This is not just my own idea. Although statistics are not available, I recently read that physicians estimate 85 percent of hospital beds in America are occupied by people with psychosomatic illnesses. A psychosomatic illness means "a physical disorder that is caused by or notably influenced by the emotional state of the patient."[5]

While there are no simple cures or quick-fixes to long-standing, emotional distresses, much benefit can be derived by forcibly changing one's outlook. The indisputable relationship between mind and body can become evident just in one's own experience.

I learned this as a small child. In our home we were

not allowed to be sick. I couldn't miss school by faking a headache or stomach distress. Because of the particular religious persuasion of our parents, we were forbidden to complain even of feeling badly.

Many times I didn't feel well enough to walk the several blocks to school, but I had no choice. By the time I arrived, I often forgot about being sick and usually had a wonderful day. My sister and I were the only students to be awarded perfect attendance certificates every year.

To this day we both are in extraordinarily good health. While I no longer embrace my parents' eccentric views, I do realize that my early training gave me the right outlook for optimal health.

Jesus Makes a Difference

It is true that the world surrounding us inflicts the most negative of atmospheres, but Christians have a choice. Nobody forces us to be part of that gloom. ". . . If I can snuggle deep into the arms of a loving God and know with overwhelming gratitude that He loves me and cares for me—how can I complain?"[6]

Jesus Christ living within makes possible a new and positive outlook.

The clouds of this world may be black and angry, but the positive influence of even one joyous believer can be like the sun peeping through those clouds. Suddenly everything is brightened, downcast spirits are lifted, and the world seems a wonderful place after all.

CHAPTER 4

Beware the Poisoned Potion

We must "develop the art of forgiveness
realizing . . . we cannot do this
unless we have divine help."[1]

Without doubt, the most difficult of all Christian disciplines is that of forgiveness. There is something deep inside which stubbornly resists extending mercy to those who trample our rights and cause us pain. And while we know what the Bible teaches about unconditional forgiveness, we become paralyzed when setting out in that direction. Perhaps the steps toward the path of forgiveness are not clear in our minds.

"I was shocked to discover," a Colorado Springs clinical psychologist recently told me, "that while researching the subject of forgiveness I could find almost nothing either in Christian materials or psychology textbooks about the process of forgiving."[2]

He went on to say that there are volumes written about God's forgiveness toward undeserving sinners, but the only thing on a personal level we are apt to hear from the pulpit is the command to forgive—no "how-to's."

Even after we decide to forgive an offending brother or sister, how do we go about it? We have chosen to do it, but what are the steps enabling us to move from decision to action? Most of us get stopped between these points.

A Painful Lesson

A few years ago a family of four lived in our community. They were sweet, precious Christians, but they were crushed under a heavy load of financial distress. They were just barely squeaking through, and not always that. It wasn't difficult to observe they were victims of their own mismanagement, but that was not the issue. They were suffering.

Right in the midst of a most critical shortage, their car broke down. We felt extremely sorry for them. The husband was hitching a ride down the mountain to work each morning. His wife, who cleaned a few houses to make extra money, walked long distances. And it was winter in Colorado.

We had two cars. Although we knew it would be a major inconvenience, we felt constrained to loan one of them for a few days until theirs was repaired. Our second car was a royal blue Volkswagen, and we had just finished a complete body overhaul. All the dents had been removed and a beautiful paint job made it look brand new. We were justly proud of it, and that was the car we decided to loan them.

We honestly rejoiced during the doubling up process. Our hearts were right, and we felt we were doing it "as unto the Lord."

A few days later the husband returned our car. We were away from home at the time, so he left it in our front parking area with a note on the windshield: "Thanks for the loan. I accidentally slid into a tree and messed up the right side. I am so sorry."

That was all. No offer to help fix it. No suggestion that as soon as he could, he would at least contribute to the cost of repair. Nothing. Period. Worse still, they never, to this day, have made reference to either our kindness in helping them or their remorse at tearing up our car.

It's probably not necessary to describe our reaction. We were stunned at first. Unbelieving. Then, slow resentment started to burn within. We felt completely justified in our resentment and even began avoiding them.

Did we ever forgive? Yes, finally.

What drove us to it? A combination of factors. We knew God couldn't honor an attitude of bitterness. We also knew we couldn't co-exist in our small community with people we refused to forgive.

More critical than either of these reasons, however, was the discovery of what was happening in our own spirits during the period we allowed resentment to build. It was like the effects of a slow poison creeping into our systems. The bitterness began with our ungrateful neighbors, but it didn't stop there. All our relationships became tainted, and a judgmental attitude set in.

Finally we came to understand why God commands His people to ". . . be kind to one another, tenderhearted, forgiving each other, just as God in Christ also has forgiven you."[3] Even though we were innocent victims and our anger could be justified, the price one pays for an unforgiving spirit is too high. No violation on earth is worth the long-range deterioration.

I only wish I could report that soon after the offense occurred, we cheerfully and immediately forgave. But we didn't. We had to simmer down, work through angry emotions, decide if we felt like forgiving or if they deserved it, and then finally get on with the mechanics of the program. It took a long time. And the relationship never was completely restored. A polite distance exists to this day.

Why Is It So Hard to Forgive?

One of the most common excuses cited is, "I really don't feel like forgiving." Naturally. Who does? I can't remember a single instance where I felt like forgiving. And if I waited until I felt like it, I'd never forgive a single soul for anything.

Forgiveness, like love, is not a feeling. It is a choice, and it involves the will rather than our emotions. One of the reasons I don't feel like forgiving is that I judge my wrongdoer as undeserving. Or I perceive myself to be innocent. Or, if I forgive, it would look as if I am condoning wrong, and I might open myself to being hurt again.

How I feel about anything is the most inaccurate measure available. For one thing, my feelings change practically every five minutes. I may feel strongly about a matter when I wake up in the morning. In a short time, I become involved with other pressing things and hardly remember my previous feelings.

During the early years of my Christian experience, I must confess that I lived almost wholly in the realm of emotions. What I felt like doing, I did. What I didn't feel like doing, I didn't. The result was the typical up-and-down syndrome so many believers complain about. Living by the dictates of emotions and doing only what feels good is a downer and wreaks havoc within the body of Christ.

So my actions must be based upon criteria more stable than my feelings. That is why I have chosen the eternal, changeless Word of God, the Bible, as my absolute guide for living. It's not always easy, and it doesn't always feel good at the moment, but when I obey God's precepts, I never fail to experience His promised "nevertheless afterwards" in the end. When I look back, I have a strong sense of satisfaction that my actions were right. Nothing brings joy like obedience to God.

Hannah Whitall Smith uses a magnificent allegory to describe the tenuous relationship between the will and the emotions.

> The will is like the wise mother of obstreperous children (the emotions). She decides on a course of action that she believes to be right. The children raise a row and say they won't have it; but the mother, knowing that she is in charge, goes calmly ahead with her plans and pays no attention to the uproar. The result is that, sooner or later, the children yield to their mother's authority and go along with her decision — and peace is restored.[4]

Must I Always Forgive?

Having determined that our emotions constitute a false criterion for behavior, and that God's Word is the only true guide, we must now discover what God actually requires.

The old human standard—"eye for eye, tooth for tooth"—reigned supreme throughout history, including Old Testament times. "If anyone injures his neighbor, whatever he has done must be done to him . . . eye for eye, tooth for tooth. As he has injured the other, so he is to be injured."[5]

By all processes of reasoning, this philosophy does seem right. If someone wrongs me, he deserves the same.

The coming of Jesus changed everything. He taught an astonishing new law, reiterated throughout the New Testament as binding upon every believer.

"You have heard that it was said, 'Eye for eye, and tooth for tooth.' But I tell you . . . if someone strikes you on the right cheek, turn to him the other also . . . if someone forces you to go one mile, go with him two miles."[6]

The apostle Peter got part of Jesus' message and understood that the old "eye for eye" standard was obsolete when he asked Him, "Lord, how many times shall I forgive my brother when he sins against me? Up to seven times?"[7]

Jesus' answer must have blown Peter's mind. No, dear Peter. Not seven times. You must forgive seventy times seven.

By simple calculation, the figure Jesus specified was 490. As far as I am concerned, He was saying to always forgive, and there are no exceptions. I have yet to forgive anyone on this earth even approaching three figures, let alone 490. That includes my husband and children combined.

What If I Don't Forgive?

For every action there must be an equal and opposite reaction. Failure to forgive begets physical as well as spiritual consequences.

Some of the spiritual effects have already been alluded to, and others will be included in this list: a critical spirit, emotional distress, hindered prayers, loss of power, impaired mental concentration, bitterness, hardness of heart. The most serious of all, however, is contained in Jesus' Sermon On The Mount: ". . . If you do not forgive men their sins, your Father will not forgive your sins."[8]

Controversy rages over the exact meaning of the last part of this verse. It is not difficult to understand why. Without even considering the doctrinal implications or translations of the original Greek text, the statement by itself is strong enough to attract careful attention. Whatever Jesus meant when He said the Father will not forgive our sins if we do not forgive our fellow Christians' sins ought to motivate us to forgive.

Not only do we suffer spiritually. Sometimes when people ask me to pray about a recurring illness, I am led to inquire, "How long has it been since you have had a private forgiving session?" The answers I receive are surprising. Guilt usually surfaces, and the resultant conversation often erupts into a tearful or angry admission of past wrongs never righted.

Am I saying illness is the result of an unforgiving spirit? Often times it is. Not all illnesses, of course. But many are. Dramatic healings often take place after a confession of long-standing resentments.

Five years ago a lady attending one of my classes became convicted of a bitter and unforgiving attitude toward her mother-in-law over an incident that had occurred eight years previously. Migraine headaches, susceptibility to recurring infections, and a borderline ulcer had begun about the same time.

When she suddenly realized the uncanny correlation between the quarrel and her continual bouts with sickness, she cried out to the Lord for mercy and humbly forgave her mother-in-law. Her symptoms disappeared, and to this day they have not returned.

Does Scriptural Forgiveness Turn Us Into Wimps?

Recently I heard a government official say on a popular television interview show that "Christians are too nice to stand up for their rights. Consequently, they are losing their battles concerning separation of church and state issues—even when the law is on their side."

Afterwards a Christian leader was asked to comment on the statement. He replied, "The terminology was most generous, but not accurate. Christians *are* wimps. Not only are they afraid to stand up for their rights, they simply won't do it."

The dialogue following these two comments highlighted a legitimate internal conflict which many sincere Christians can't seem to resolve. We are taught to turn the other cheek and go the second mile. So where do we draw the line between clear New Testament teaching on forbearance and forgiveness as opposed to needful confrontation?

The truth is, we can thoroughly forgive someone's offense and still see the need for confrontation. It is sad to note that the actual word *confront* carries a completely negative implication. It need not be so. If executed according to scriptural directives, confrontation can be a thoroughly positive encounter.

While doing an extensive writing assignment a few years ago for a prominent Christian leader, I became aware that I was losing my creative edge and dreaded continuing the project. I mentally conjured up every imaginable excuse to renege, fully knowing it wasn't possible.

For several months I had realized something was drastically wrong, but instead of being objective and searching out reasons, I remained subjective and took everything personally. The more unwarranted the pressure he exerted upon me and the less cooperative he became, the more I blamed myself—for not wanting to finish what I agreed to do, for mediocrity, and for being unjustly critical in my heart.

When the situation reached a crucial impasse, I sought counsel. It was impossible for me to think clearly. In fact, I became so incapacitated that I wondered if I might be suffering some kind of breakdown.

It didn't take a counselor long to evaluate the situation and determine the problem was not mine. It was my employer's, and what was needed was a scriptural confrontation.

Carefully outlining the way to do it, this godly helper directed me in planning and executing the session. After intensive prayer for two days, I went. What transpired was the most amazing experience.

God had prepared my employer's heart the night before by revealing hidden pockets of anger due to problems in other areas of his life. He had been venting his frustrations toward his family, his secretaries, and his staff. I was merely one of the scapegoats. Neither he nor I fully understood what was happening, but the Holy Spirit did. And the moment I began to pray and determined that I would gather my courage and face the issue, God stepped in to resolve it.

The final result? I was able to complete the project, and my employer was spiritually healed and renewed.

The scriptural basis for the action I used was found in Galatians 6:1: "Brethren, if a man is overtaken in a fault, you which are spiritual should restore such a one in the spirit of meekness (gentleness) . . ."

The key to the entire process is found in the word "restore." The purpose for constructive confrontation is to restore, not to vent one's anger or to punish the wrongdoer. If restoration is the sincere motive, everything else will fall into place.

Just a few suggestions are in order here:

- Before confronting, be certain of your motives. Clear your heart of anger.

- Pray earnestly that God will prepare both you and your "confrontee." Do not go until you know God's timing is right.

- Prepare a written outline of what you plan to say. Memorize certain key statements and practice your delivery.

- Do not accuse or blame. Use your own perceptions and feelings as a basis for presentation. (Use "I" statements instead of "you.")

For instance, my opening remark was, "I need to tell you that I am experiencing great difficulty with my work. I have been feeling lately that something is wrong in our relationship, and I have come to the conclusion that I will be unable to finish this project unless things change."

That was all I needed to say. I had it carefully memorized so I wouldn't accidentally blurt out the wrong thing. The Lord took over from there and resolved the whole situation.

Is There an Easy Way to Forgive?

If there is, I haven't found it. The only thing I can say is the more you do it, the easier it gets. "Practice makes perfect" applies in the spiritual realm as well as the physical.

Analyzing what happens when someone trespasses against us, I have come to understand that the order of occurrence is rather predictable:

First, a hurtful event transpires causing a loss of self-esteem. Or a violation of personal rights or property occurs.

Second, an emotional response results—usually anger, hurt feelings, or self-pity.

Third, a choice follows.

Fourth, the fruit of that decision begins to grow.

The choice indicated in the third step of the above sequence is limited to three options. First, we can choose to suppress our anger and do nothing outwardly. Just let it burn within. This method of handling offenses is like a dam whose water continually piles up until it overflows or bursts through the restrictive walls. Anger eventually erupts somewhere — either physically in ourselves or to the other person.

Second, we can ignore our anger. While this is another form of suppression, it is more passive and places us in a position to go either way. People with high self-esteem and who are not worried about their rights can more easily ignore injustices. While this method is superior to the first, it is not God's highest purpose for His children.

The third option is always the best. We can choose to forgive. The fruit of this choice precipitates a waning of feelings and an ultimate forgetting. Forgiveness is God's method and it pleases Him.

Workable Steps to Forgiveness

Each person is a distinctly different creation from God's hand. No two of us are alike. This means what works for me might not work for you. Therefore, I do not say this is a fool-proof formula. The following is merely a suggested outline to help you gain perspective when working through to forgiveness.

1. After the offense has occurred, in the heat of the moment, try to *avoid contact* with the offender and remain neutral.

2. *Get alone*, review the offense and begin to balance your outlook. Ask yourself, Is this a personal attack, or is it not? Many times we perceive an offense when it really isn't. I think of instances when my husband has said something to me which I take personally and misconstrue as a personal affront. When finally I confront him, he is astonished. "I can't believe you thought that," he says. "That was the farthest thing from my mind."

3. Adopt a position of *empathy*. Try to understand why the person acted or spoke as he did. Put yourself in his

place and examine all the contributing factors. You might decide that, given the identical circumstances, you would have done the same thing.

4. If you still fail to gain perspective, it may be helpful to *talk to another person*. This is a "dumping" of feelings. Be careful to choose someone you trust implicitly, and who is committed to godly counsel rather than partisan diplomacy. A pastor qualifies well. Sometimes you do not need advice. Just a listening ear to spill out feelings. Other times both counsel and prayer are essential.

5. *Pray.* The reason I have chosen this order is that in the heat of anger, I cannot pray. Probably I should be more spiritual, but I am not. So when anger subsides and perspective is restored, then God's supernatural power through answered prayer can open our hearts.

Confession of personal sin is necessary at this point. For me, it is important to distance myself from the offense by realizing I am not responsible for the sins of others against me. I am responsible, however, for my reaction to those sins. If I react in anger, then I must confess my anger and trust God to forgive me.

6. *Forgive.* Finally you are ready to pray for your errant brother or sister. Whether you feel like it or not, verbalize your forgiveness to God. It helps me to speak audibly. "Father, in the name of Jesus, I forgive _____. I choose to obey you instead of clinging to my rights."

Forgiveness is the surrendering of my right to hold a grudge against anyone no matter how justified I am. This step may involve talking to the offender in order to save the relationship. One word of caution here. If you've resolved your anger and have thoroughly forgiven your offender, do not verbally apologize for your feelings of unforgiveness unless harm has been inflicted upon that person.

People have come to me at times to apologize for their unforgiveness when I didn't even know I had offended them. One such lady rushed up to me after a church service and said, "Oh, Madalene, please forgive me for harboring resentment in my heart toward you."

I was stunned. As far as I knew, our relationship was good.

"What for, Jaunita?" I asked.

"Well, I'm ashamed to tell you. But after your daughter, Lenee, gave birth to her baby, and I heard you didn't even get up in the middle of the night to help her, I just got so angry with you."

"But Jaunita, Lenee nursed her baby. What could I do if I got up in the night? My part was to take care of Michael all day long while Lenee slept."

"Well, I just thought you should have gotten up in case she needed you. But I have confessed my resentment to the Lord, and now I apologize to you."

7. Choose to *never speak of the offense to anyone.* Ask the Lord to put a guard on your mouth.

8. *Discard the memory* by interrupting your thoughts whenever you start rehearsing the event. This works for any wrong thought patterns. I simply say out loud, "Stop it!" and immediately replace the destructive thoughts with positive ones.

Why Forgive?

God commands it. The Bible teaches it. You need it. Your offender needs it.

Most of all, the Lord Jesus gloriously exemplified what forgiveness is all about when He made His supreme sacrifice on Calvary's cross. Think about it. Jesus was the only person on earth to live a spotless life. No finger could point to Him and accuse Him of wrongdoing.

When cruel men nailed Him to the cross, they committed the most diabolically vicious sin ever to be recorded in history's annals. Their evil hearts inflicted excruciating agony upon the perfect Son of God.

What was His response?

He looked down from that torturous instrument of death and loved them. In no other way could He have spoken such immortal words: "Father, forgive them. They don't even know what they're doing."

If Jesus could forgive those who put Him to death without cause, can we not follow His example?

CHAPTER 5

Don't Get in My Way

"God does not coerce us to follow Him.
He invites us . . .
He wills our freedom to decline or to accept."[1]

"I don't know what to do with this child," I moaned. "He is so strong-willed that I simply can't handle him."

He was two, and weren't two-year-olds supposed to be impossible? That was about all I knew of child rearing. We didn't have James Dobson in those days to identify this child as strong-willed and to give us helpful information on how to deal with him.

As God would arrange it, however, I made the above statement in the company of a wise and godly woman, Mary Herring. As soon as I said it, she turned to me and quietly asked: "Madalene, are you just going to hand this child over to the devil?"

If she meant to shock me, she did. "Of course not!" I cried. "I have committed this child to the Lord. I want him to live for God's glory."

"Then you must break his strong will."

"Break it?" I objected. "But I thought that would create emotional damage for the rest of his life."

"You are speaking of the spirit," she carefully explained. "You must never break a child's spirit. But you must break the stubborn will that says 'I'm going to do what I want to do, not what you want me to do.' "

"If you don't," she continued, "you will encounter serious discipline problems during teenage years, and he will become a rebellious adult for the rest of his life."

"I didn't dream it was that serious," I replied. "But isn't it hard to break a child's will?"

"Think of it as similar to the handle of a fragile china teacup. Often those handles become broken, and if it is an expensive set, we carefully glue it back on. Once it is broken, however, it is always subject to being easily broken again. A child's will is the same."

Looking back upon that lengthy conversation and the help Mary gave me in dealing with my child, I now realize that many of today's problems among both youth and adults relate directly to what she said. Self-willed, rebellious people, accustomed to having their way and yielding to no one, keep the world in turmoil, to say nothing of the entire body of Christ.

What, Actually, Is Rebellion?

Although the dictionary defines rebellion as "resistance to or defiance of any authority, control, or tradition,"[2] my friend Mary put it in understandable "Americanese." Rebellion, she said, is the attitude that says, "I'm going to do *what* I want to do *when* I want to do it, and *nobody* can stop me." It may be verbal or non-verbal.

In our society we associate rebellion with teenagers, drugs, alcohol, illicit or perverted sex, and abuse of all kinds. As long as it is confined to such designations, those of us who do not indulge in those excesses often consider ourselves "off-the-hook."

Although rebellion is unquestionably the spiritual disease of our day, we have a wrong concept concerning its manifestation. "It's in the kids," we quickly note. But we must remember that rebellion is an inner condition. Outward actions merely denote the inner source.

C.S. Lewis wrote: "If anyone thinks that Christians regard unchastity as the supreme vice, he is quite wrong. Sins of the flesh are bad, but they are the least bad of all sins . . . a cold, self-righteous prig who goes regularly to church may be far nearer to hell than a prostitute. But, of course, it is better to be neither."[3]

Is it possible to appear righteous, be a church leader, know the language, look spiritual, and still be a rebel? Tragically, people get saved and bring their old rebellious attitudes into church. Sometimes I think spiritual rebels are the worst. Certainly they are the hardest to get at because they know all the coverups.

Doing My Own Thing

Why are believers often defeated and miserable? Why are churches today in such turmoil? My speaking and counseling ministry takes me to churches and groups throughout the United States and abroad. I must admit that often I am thoroughly disheartened with what I find. A few notable exceptions exist, but the vast majority of evangelical bodies are either dead or dying of a creeping malignancy. Usually the pastor is too busy dealing with symptoms to get at the real cause.

The truth is, God has been after something in us for years—and we have resisted. We manage to always "wiggle out" of situations where we have to do what we don't want to do. We are escape artists, pros at evasion, and we know all the right Scripture verses to cover up our true motives. As a result, our Christian life has been hard, and we haven't understood why.

The Problem—Then and Now

Jesus said, "Why do you call me 'Lord, Lord,' and do not do what I say?"[4]

What was He talking about? What was the big problem in Jesus' day? Interestingly, it parallels our own.

It was this: The people were very religious, but they

never obeyed. They couldn't comprehend that there is a difference between being religious and obeying God.

Let us go even further. Not only is there a difference between religion and obedience, but there is a difference between outward spirituality and faithfulness versus obedience. Strangely, most Christians have trouble distinguishing between these elements.

So we suppose if we are faithful in church attendance, do our daily Bible readings, and pray now and then, that's all there is to obeying God. Our biggest concerns are what we do rather than who we are.

When people come to me for counsel and I discern this is their problem, I am forced to say, "Please don't tell me with your mouth that you want to please God, while your everyday choices indicate you are going to do exactly what you want to do. You are being totally inconsistent with God's Word."

This is precisely what Jesus meant when He said, in essence, "Don't call me Lord if you refuse to do the things I say." So the believer who professes Jesus as Lord but does not live in obedience is a rebel.

Two things happen as a result of this misplaced emphasis:

1. The non-Christian person who watches the average church member comes to the conclusion that Christianity consists of doing things for God. So our churches fill up with people who do not understand the doctrine of salvation.

2. Many of those who do have a genuine rebirth by receiving Jesus Christ as personal Savior eventually get caught up in the machinery of the "works syndrome." Then they suffer burnout, nervous breakdown, or early spiritual demise and walk away forever.

Either way, not only does the church suffer, but the cause of Christ as a whole becomes weakened. That's when "little fires" start kindling and draw attention away from our main objective.

Are We Saved to Serve?

Often we hear the statement, "We are saved to serve." Sounds pretty good, doesn't it? But are we? Perhaps confusion exists because of the Scripture, "faith without works is dead."[5]

My problem is that I am a people-pleaser. I end up serving people. Whatever they ask me to do, I'm afraid to say no. So if I don't have a better understanding of the purpose of my salvation, I am liable to be in big trouble before I know it. And just for the record, I've been in that kind of trouble. I know what it is.

What, Then, Is the Christian's Goal?

The ultimate in Christian living is not doing things for God. It is, instead, finding the will of God and doing it.

Charles Swindoll made a statement over the radio one day: "The goal of the Christian life is not happiness. It is to glorify God. If happiness comes, that's just the cream on the pie."

The Bible says, "Glorify God in your body and in your spirit, which are God's."[6] If we ever really grasped this principle, a great many problems Christians face today could be resolved.

For instance, we thought we were getting married to be happy, didn't we? So when we are not happy, we begin to find excuses to leave the marriage. I'm not faulting happiness within marriage. It's wonderful if we are supremely happy, but that's not the goal. Glorifying God is. If my focus in life is how I can better glorify God, problems within my marriage will eventually dissipate.

We thought we were joining a church to be happy, didn't we? So if the least murmur of disagreement occurs, we are ready to pack up and find another one more to our liking. Trouble is, we keep running from church to church because each one is filled with imperfect people. Also because we misunderstood the true goal of the Christian life.

Delegated Authority Brings Out Rebellion

Often I hear people say, "I want only God to rule over me. Nobody else." We can keep God at a respectable distance, so that's pretty safe, isn't it?

The Bible teaches, however, that all authority is from God. The apostle Paul makes this quite clear:

> Everyone must submit himself to the governing authorities, for there is no authority except that which God has established. The authorities that exist have been established by God. Consequently, he who rebels against the authority is rebelling against what God has instituted.[7]

Rebellion surfaces when God sends delegated authority. Parent over child. Employer over employee. Pastor over church. And in order to rationalize an unyielding refusal to submit, one of the first things a rebel does is find fault with his authority: "I walked by my pastor's house and heard him yelling at his wife. I can't submit to a man like that."

So a rebel doesn't submit to his pastor because he doesn't do things right. Or to civil authorities because they don't do things right. Or wife to a husband, because he's not spiritual enough. Or to the president, because he's from the opposition party.

Once we start down this selective road of submitting only to those authorities we feel deserving of it, we miss the whole point of God's plan for order. Nobody is fully deserving. Nobody is perfect. And certainly there will be abuses.

If, however, we do not recognize the need to find our authorities and submit to them, chaos will result. And that's exactly what now exists in many nations, areas of our own government, public schools, churches, and business organizations.

A rebel is a manipulator—forever fighting, spiteful and unloving. He must always be in control of every situation—so when things go wrong, he can blame others.

The bottom-line motive of the rebel is control—of his own life, those around him, and every situation related to him. Anyone who disagrees with him automatically becomes his enemy, and he spends much of his time in verbal combat. Manipulating becomes a way of life.

It's a Matter of Pride

The question is not, *Are we rebels?* We all are. But as Christians, we must discover to what extent rebellion rules our lives. Our humanistic society nurtures this spirit beginning with toddlers as they watch Saturday morning cartoons. If you don't believe it, parents, get up early and join the kids.

And it doesn't stop in the nursery. Our educational system supports the process, women's lib groups promote it further, and the appealing "macho" emphasis builds the male ego until no one considers himself/herself normal without a strong spirit of rebellion.

People often say with great pride, "Oh, I'm just a rebel at heart. I've always been known to be one."

We think it's cute in little children when they exhibit early signs of sassiness or insubordination. "He's just like his grandpa, so independent you can't tell him anything."

In the church, of course, we do not label ourselves as rebellious. We use less offensive terms such as determined, strong-willed, sharpminded, clever, successful, assertive. If we knew the truth, we would realize that others probably think of us in less complimentary terms.

An Incurable Rebel

Saul, King of Israel, is a choice illustration of total rebellion. His story is told in 1 Samuel 15.

The prophet Samuel was God's delegated spiritual authority. Through Samuel, God instructed Saul that he was to punish the Amalekites for their sins against Israel by attacking and killing all the people, cattle, sheep, camels and donkeys.

Saul obediently went. He led his forces against the enemy and overcame them. He did kill all the people, cattle, sheep, camels and donkeys — except for their king and the choicest of their animals. That seemed reasonable, didn't it? So Saul did what he wanted to do when he wanted to do it, and nobody could stop him. He was the king!

When he returned home, Samuel confronted him and asked him why he hadn't obeyed. Note Saul's responses:

1. I obeyed (verse 13).

2. "The soldiers . . . spared the best of the sheep and cattle . . . But we totally destroyed the rest" (verse 15).

3. "But I did obey the Lord . . . the soldiers . . ." (verses 20-21).

4. "I have sinned . . . I was afraid . . . forgive my sin and come back with me, so that I may worship the Lord" (verses 24-25).

Why didn't God forgive Saul when he said, "I have sinned?" He forgave those same words when King David later spoke them. The reason God refused to forgive Saul was because deep inside of him was an attitude of rebellion, a core of resistance that couldn't be broken. David, on the other hand, knew how to break. When confronted with his sin, he immediately said, "I'm the man. I know I am." If you want to see how to break, read Psalm 51.

Where to Begin?

I honestly believe most of the dilemmas Christians and churches face in this generation stem from one root cause: rebellion. The outward symptoms may vary, but the source is the same.

Before a disease can be treated, accurate diagnosis of the condition must be made and accepted by the patient. If we deal merely with symptoms, curing the disease is impossible. Band-aids won't touch this deep internal malady called rebellion. Only radical surgery will do the job.

It will be necessary, therefore, to face and admit the diagnosis. A defensive attitude prolongs the malady, and while rebellion rules a human heart, God's peace cannot permeate the thick layers of insulation.

Like Saul and David, every believer has these same four choices when confronted:

1. Give the stock answers to skirt the issue. ("I *have* obeyed.")

2. Blame someone else. ("The people did it.")

"It's my husband's fault."

"It's my pastor. I can't be spiritual because I don't get fed at my church."

"My children keep me from doing God's will."

3. Keep up the front even when you know you are wrong. Try to keep others from finding out. ("Come worship with me, Samuel, so no one will know.")

4. Break. Immediately admit and confess the sin of rebellion. ("I am the man.")

Oswald Chambers writes beautifully of the blessed result of obedience: "The Lord does not give me rules, He makes His standard very clear, and if my relationship to Him is that of love, I will do what He says without any hesitation . . . when I do obey Him, I fulfill my spiritual destiny."[8]

PART TWO

Finding the Best Route

The seasoned mountain climber quickly discovers that a trail map is his most trustworthy companion. He spends long hours studying it so he may find the best routes. As he marks the trails, he carefully plans for needed provisions along the way. If he circumvents these vital procedures, he knows he can easily be lost.

CHAPTER 6

I Pray For a Thirst

*"If we had a real inkling
of the power of the Word of God,
we would spend more time in it."*[1]

What makes some people old before their time while others retain youthfulness, vitality, and optimism into their 80s and 90s? Personally, I do not believe youthfulness is restricted to the physical body. The present emphasis upon keeping the exterior young deludes us in the pursuit of true youth — that of the spirit.

Let me tell you about a man who gave me his secret. He is ninety-six years old at this writing. You'd expect him to be in a nursing home by now, but he is far from that scene. He regularly teaches in a Bible College, still travels extensively as a speaker for Bible conferences and retreats, maintains a daily radio program, and is the most hopeful, alive and alert human being I know.

He is Dr. John G. Mitchell, founder of Multnomah School of the Bible in Portland, Oregon. God used this man to bring my entire family to the Savior. At that time we were steeped in a religious cult. I was seventeen years old and knew all the answers to all the questions. But God worked in unbelievable ways to open our eyes and hearts to the gospel.

By the time I became a believer, I enjoyed slightly

more than a year under Dr. Mitchell's teaching before leaving for college. Following my first year at Wheaton College, I stayed home to study the Bible at Multnomah, returning the next year to Wheaton. Except for my wedding and my father's funeral, I did not see Dr. Mitchell again. After fifteen years of marriage and four children, I learned one summer that he would be the main conference speaker at Glen Eyrie in Colorado Springs. We lived just two hours from Glen Eyrie.

That same week our children were scheduled to attend church camp. With eager anticipation I made plans to drop them off and journey on to Colorado Springs to sit under Dr. Mitchell's teaching once again. I must admit I was curious to see what he looked like after all this time. He was seventy some years old by then, and I thought (foolishly) that this might be the last time I'd ever see him.

When I arrived and walked into the registration area, he was surrounded by people waiting to talk to him. I couldn't believe my eyes! He didn't appear to have aged a bit since I had last seen him in my early twenties. Knowing, however, that *I* had changed considerably during those years, before approaching him I tried to think of some way to make myself known without embarrassing him. Surely he wouldn't recognize me.

While my mind was busily occupied working out my plan, suddenly he caught sight of me, whirled around, pointed a finger and said, "It was on a Tuesday night, and we were studying the book of Hebrews." My mouth must have dropped wide open. Not only did he recognize me—he also remembered the night I received Christ.

Watching him during that week, I was astounded at his energy. I resolved to approach him when he was alone to ask his formula for staying young. My opportunity came toward the end of the week.

"Dr. Mitchell, please tell me how you remain so vigorous and dynamic at your age? I'd like to start practicing."

"Magdalene [always his special name for me], it's the Word. I pray daily for a thirst for the Word of God."

He paused a few seconds. My mind clutched at his statement, and I thought, *That's it! I must pray more for a thirst.* Then he continued. "But thirst or not, I discipline myself and get into the Word whether I feel like it or not."

Probably he doesn't know what a lasting impact his statement made upon me. I must admit that I find myself more often in the "or not" category. I love it when I eagerly thirst for the Word of God and can hardly wait to open its pages. But that is the exception rather than the rule.

Spiritual Malnourishment—Disease of the Church

I feel safe in saying that most Christians are like me. We operate on a thirst schedule, and if we aren't thirsty, we figure we can dispense with the routine of reading the Bible. No wonder we move spiritually at a snail's pace. No wonder we suffer from inner hunger and lack power to overcome the evil one.

As a teacher and conference speaker for many years, I have counseled a great many people who come to me with spiritual problems. First, I listen to them. When they are finished, almost always I ask the same question: "Tell me, are you in the Word of God every day? Is God speaking to you on a regular basis?"

Usually the answer goes something like this: "I know I ought to be, but I haven't been lately." Or, "I haven't felt much like reading the Bible." Or, "Honestly, I've been so busy I just don't have time." Please don't misunderstand me. I am not saying that the believer who daily feeds upon God's Word is magically exempt from life's crushing ordeals. Jesus Himself said "in the world you will find tribulation." But He quickly added, "Be of good cheer, for I have overcome the world."[2] We have power through Him to rise above the tribulations of the world. How do we do it?

Let's use a common, everyday analogy. Most

Americans find time to fit in three meals a day. From all appearances, many of us exceed that standard by a long shot. Whether we have time or not, whether we feel like it or not, we still eat. If we neglect nourishment, we know we will become weak and unable to accomplish our daily tasks. So we don't miss it.

Spiritually it's the same thing. Jesus said, "I am the bread of life. He who comes to me will never go hungry..."[3] From a purely practical standpoint, I know of only one way to eat the bread Jesus spoke about—feed on God's Word.

What Happens When We Don't?

- Lack of power. We discover that the cutting edge of our ability to overcome evil is diminished.

- Weakness in resisting temptation. Things that formerly were easy to resist become snares.

- Muddled, confused objectives. "The entrance of Thy Word gives light," the psalmist said. Without that light from above, we cannot see clearly enough to avoid tripping over avoidable obstacles.

- Absence of joy and peace. The heart becomes heavy and overwrought. A formerly light and happy spirit is replaced by an "uptight" demeanor.

Because I have lived long enough to experience all of the above, I never ask myself in the morning whether there is time to read the Bible. I remember the code Watchman Nee lived by: "No Bible, no breakfast."

I realize this is not easy when children are in the home. Or when you are rushing to work early each morning. However, the pursuit of spiritual maturity is not to be found on the fast, easy lane of life. The world system will never be geared to the believer's quiet time schedule. There is only one way to get the time: take it by force. The rewards for setting an early alarm in order to be with God are innumerable.

One of my beloved nieces, Jenny, lives with

numerous problems serious enough to drive most of us to utter despair. If you knew her circumstances, you'd say, "Whew! I thought I had troubles."

But Jenny is always upbeat in attitude. This is not because she was born a happy person, but because she has discovered the spring of joy: time with God each morning. She sets her alarm for 4:45 A.M. to arise before the mad scramble of getting children off to school.

"My quiet time is the absolute highlight of my day," Jenny says. "During those incredibly dark hours, I discovered that time with the Lord is an absolute necessity if I'm going to find enough strength to walk wherever my path takes me."

Because of her persistent, daily poring over the pages of Scripture, she is becoming authoritative in understanding and interpreting truth.

God's Word Keeps Us Clean

"Now you are clean through the Word which I have spoken unto you."[4]

It's like taking a bath on the inside. It reminds me of the times I hike on the dusty Rocky Mountain trails surrounding our home. Usually I don't stick to the designated paths or roads. I'd rather strike off into a lovely aspen grove or a pine forest. Or climb huge rock formations. When I return home, always I am sweaty, thirsty, and ready for a shower. I cannot describe the tingling exhilaration afterwards.

The same thing happens with the daily reading of God's Word. All of the tiredness and accumulated grime from our weary pilgrimage on this earth is washed away. We experience a renewed spirit as we arise refreshed, no matter how burdensome the struggles and heartaches of yesterday.

Specifically, how does this take place? Sin, whether in the life of a believer or unbeliever, deposits guilt within the spirit. We can rationalize it away in our minds, or we can pay a psychiatrist to tell us we are not guilty—but guilt remains because it is not a mental function. Guilt is registered in the spirit, so my mind cannot convince my spirit that I am not guilty.

Let's consider one of the most prevalent and accepted sins of our day—sexual promiscuity. God, who knows how He created the human body and who ordained its every function perfectly, warned us against the sins of adultery, fornication, homosexuality and the like.

Now it doesn't matter how much effort we exert to justify, condone, or ignore these sins. We can mentally assure ourselves that the old taboos no longer apply. We can fill our minds with the "facts" propagated by the strong humanistic philosophy of our day (i.e., that it is not wrong or sinful to indulge natural impulses with which we were born and which our nature demands).

But God says sex outside of marriage is sin. And if the current epidemic of social diseases isn't enough to persuade us, the irreparably damaged lives and emotions of those caught in the flood of this lifestyle ought to say something.

An interesting sidelight exists. Those involved in promiscuous sex repeatedly assert that it is no different from satisfying other bodily needs. Why, then, should they experience guilt feelings? Yet the first thing to happen when these same people receive Jesus Christ as personal Savior is a complete recall of all their "normal" behavior, followed by agonizing repentance and great relief from the forgiveness of guilt feelings they said they never had.

God's Word Is Like a Mirror to Correct our Conduct

"Anyone who listens to the Word but does not do what it says is like a man who looks at his face in a mirror and, after looking at himself goes away and immediately forgets what he looks like."[5]

I laugh as I recall times when I felt good about my appearance, then accidentally glanced into a mirror to discover with horror that my hair was disheveled, or my lipstick smeared. "Surely I haven't looked like this all morning!" is my shocked reaction.

Similarly, I have often felt good about myself spiritually, how I am handling situations, how I am growing, and how fortunate my church and my world are to have a wonderful Christian like me. Then I open God's Word, and I am appalled to discover how far short I am falling.

Recently this happened to me. I was reading the Bible when a verse jumped out and grabbed my attention. It said: "Do not let any unwholesome talk come out of your mouths, but only what is helpful for building others up according to their needs, that it might benefit those who listen."[6]

Suddenly the spotlight beamed on my verbal communications. I had been angry with my husband that morning, and although I didn't lash out in temper, I knew my spiteful words had not built him up or benefited him. At the time I felt justified, because I knew he was wrong. Nevertheless, I sensed my need for repentance and determined to guard my mouth all day so I would not face bitter regrets by nightfall. (Funny thing . . . when I allowed the Lord to soften my heart, I realized my husband wasn't as wrong as I had thought.)

When God's Word convicts us, we have a choice. Either we can correct our conduct, or we can continue as if we had never looked at ourselves. But we cannot receive this correction apart from daily gazing into God's mirror and subsequently mending the flaws.

God's Word Lights Up Our Path

"Your Word is a lamp to my feet, a light to my path."[7]

My husband uses a beautiful illustration of this verse. In the days when it was written, no flashlights, street lamps, or automobile headlights pierced the thick darkness of night. Without a full moon, a night walker could easily stumble over unseen obstacles.

To prevent this, he strapped a round-shaped rock on his foot whose center was carefully chipped out. Within the cavity of the rock a pitch-like substance called bitumine was placed and ignited with fire.

As the night traveler walked, the small flame illumined a circle of light. All he could safely see was the next step. So he walked with head down and eyes fastened upon the small lighted area about his feet.

The psalmist was referring to that ancient custom when he told us God's Word is a lamp for our feet. If we fail to strap that lamp on each day, we cannot see to take the next step. That's why we so often stumble.

God didn't promise He would spread out a blueprint of our whole lives before us. But He did promise to illumine each step as we keep our eyes upon Him.

A Step Further

After years of daily reading God's Word, I discovered a secret that absolutely revolutionized my spiritual walk. As simply as I can, I want to tell you about it.

One day I was reading and meditating upon Psalm 1. Replacing the word "man" with "woman," I read:

> Blessed is the woman who walks not in the counsel of the ungodly, nor stands in the way of the sinner, nor sits in the seat of the scornful. But her delight is in the law [Word] of the Lord, and in His law [Word] does she meditate day and night. She shall be like a tree planted by the rivers of water that brings forth her fruit in her season. Her leaf also shall not wither, and whatever she does will prosper.

The last line caught my attention. If there was anything in life I wanted, it was to prosper in all my endeavors. So I retraced my steps through this psalm to the original condition attached to this unbelievable promise. There it was. All I had to do was "meditate day and night" in God's Word.

I knew how to do this during the waking hours of the day. As long as my conscious mind was functioning, all I needed were determination and discipline to review and enjoy God's Word.

But what about night when I was asleep? How in the world does one meditate on God's Word in the dead of night? Only one way. Scripture memorization.

It wasn't that I hadn't memorized. In fact, I had systematically memorized and regularly reviewed the entire Topical Memory System.[8] One aspect of the discipline I had never attempted, however, was to memorize entire chapters. Somehow the thought of such a task terrified me. But now, eager to put God to the test and discover how to prosper in everything I did, I decided to memorize whole chapters at a time.

I began with Psalm 1. Since it contained only six verses, I figured I could handle this little chapter without too much difficulty. Besides, whenever I reviewed it, I would be reminded again of my goal — prospering.

From there I moved to Psalm 37:1-11. After six verses, I felt it wise not to bite off too large a chunk for the second round. I might run the risk of becoming discouraged, and I really wanted to succeed.

As God would plan it, during the Psalm 37 exercise a great trial engulfed me. Usually a sound sleeper, I now lay awake most of the night sifting through each detail of the ordeal facing me. After stumbling through a couple of weary days from not sleeping, it dawned on me that if I reviewed my memorized chapters while lying awake, my attention might be diverted.

It worked! I have no idea how quickly I fell asleep that first night. But I awakened refreshed and able to trust God in a new way. Didn't Psalm 37 say that if I delighted myself in the Lord, I would receive the desires of my heart? And you can't imagine how quickly God resolved my "impossible" situation.

Finally I understood how to meditate on God's

Word both day and night. Since that time, I don't mind waking up in the middle of the night. Only God knows the hours of enraptured communion I have spent with Him while everyone else is sound asleep.

Shared Blessings

Whenever possible, I try to share with others the priceless lessons I learn from the Lord. Often, my niece is first in line simply because she has such an open and teachable spirit, and because she lives nearby and is as close as my telephone.

My opportunity came when she, too, was engulfed in several huge trials. It hadn't been too long since my Psalm 37 ordeal, so the memory was fresh in my mind.

While we were talking on the telephone one day, I told her about my newest blessing—middle-of-the-night Scripture meditation.

"I want you to do something for me," I told her. "In fact, this is an assignment, not an option. Please memorize the first eleven verses of Psalm 37 and constantly review them during these dark days and nights."

Here is what happened, in Jenny's own words: "At first I did it only because I promised. Our circumstances had become desperate, and I was willing to try anything. Still I had no notion it would be more than a mental exercise.

"In just a few days of working on Psalm 37, my heavy heart became unexplainably light. Nothing had changed as far as our situation. In fact, things were getting worse. But my heart was not dragging the pits anymore.

"My family couldn't understand me—neither could I, for that matter. They acted almost as if they resented my lighthearted attitude and told me I should be more distraught and concerned about our hopeless condition. But I became so joyful in the Lord that I could hardly wait to see how He planned to solve our problems.

"Now I memorize Scripture because I can't live

without it. The Word of God has become 'my meat and drink,' so to speak. Nothing has ever affected my life so deeply."

It Really Works!

Since my early experiences in memorizing chapters of the Bible, I have recommended this practice wherever I speak. Those who have tried it echo my testimony that nothing has ever affected my life so deeply.

Here are some suggestions to help you get started.

1. Begin by memorizing a short chapter—such as Psalm 1. You will be encouraged that you can indeed master something you formerly thought impossible.

2. Do not set deadlines, but discipline yourself to work at least ten minutes each day. Simply work on new material each day while reviewing completed portions, and move at your own pace.

3. Use "dead" times to review, such as when driving alone, standing in lines, ironing, sewing or lying awake at night.

4. Consider Scripture memorization as a way of life—not a mental exercise to be dropped after you have accomplished a few chapters.

5. Do not memorize with the idea of "performing." This is between you and the Lord. He is your audience.

6. A few key chapters I have memorized: John 14, John 15, Romans 6, Romans 8, 1 Peter 1, 1 Corinthians 1:18 through 2, Philippians 3, 2 Corinthians 4, Psalms 1, 19, 25, 103, 139. These might give you ideas for starters.

CHAPTER 7

Discovering Secret Paths

*"Prayer does not fit us for the greater works;
Prayer is the greater work."*[1]

Christians love to talk about prayer. It is a favorite topic for meetings and discussion groups. Sadly, though, Christians love to talk about prayer, but few actually pray.

Often people tell me their problems and ask that I pray for them. Then they add, "God has given you unusual prayer power. You can get through while others cannot."

I'd like to address that statement: Baloney! It's a lie, it's unscriptural, and it's a cop-out.

God has no favorites. He did not say, "If you ask anything in my name, I will do it—but this is just for you, Madalene, and a few selected others." How absurd. His limitless power is for every child of God. And there are no exceptions.

The only difference is that some have stopped talking about it and are doing it. That's why they seem to have a direct line to heaven. The indisputable fact is that every believer has equal access.

The Pervasiveness of Prayer

Prayer is the greatest weapon we possess. We are told it is "mighty through God to the pulling down of strongholds."[2]

Jesus said, "Whatever you ask in my name, that will I do that the Father may be glorified in the Son. If you ask anything in my name, I will do it."[3]

Exactly what did Jesus mean when He said "anything"? To answer that question, may I suggest that you look up all the references in the Bible containing the word *prayer*. You will quickly note the unlimited nature of God's promises—"anything," "everything," "whatsoever," "what things soever,"—no limit.

More people waste time trying to explain away or qualify the all-inclusive scope of God's prayer promises than those who take advantage of them. It is as if they are trying to save face for a decadent church, or justify their own powerlessness before God.

I do not propose to untangle the theological knots concerning the *whatsoevers* and *anythings*. For myself, I have come to the position of merely believing that God will do precisely what He says He will do.

Does "Anything" Include Material Things?

A few years ago my husband learned he had cancer. Ironically, we had just embarked on a faith ministry, and we were desperately in need of a more dependable car. Our situation looked hopeless. No salary, a sick husband, and two older-model, ailing automobiles.

Someone loaned me a copy of a book about faith. If I ever needed anything at that time, I needed faith. The book, however, was not the usual theological treatise. It was a simple, down-to-earth practical application of God's Word.

One of the exercises at the end of a chapter designed to stimulate faith was to write down a list of five things I needed, give God a time limit, and trust Him to provide those five things within that time limit. The prescribed promise to claim was, "My God shall supply all your need."[4]

I gasped! *Give God a time limit? What audacity,* I thought. Certainly I had never been guilty of that.

For several days, though, I couldn't get that daring challenge off my mind. We desperately needed a dependable car. Couldn't God provide His children with material necessities? Didn't He say He would supply all our needs?

Finally I rolled a sheet of paper in to my typewriter, took a deep breath, and wrote:

> October 16, 1980
> On this day, in accordance with God's promise to supply all our need, I am believing God to replace our old car with a more dependable, later model that gives better gas mileage. I am trusting Him to give it to us in three months from this date.
> Signed: _____

Please note that I didn't have courage to ask for a new car. Only a later model. Also, I couldn't ask for five things. One was all I could manage.

To inform my husband of this wild leap of faith, I decided to thank God for the car during our morning prayers. When we finished, he looked at me for a long moment of silence.

"Don't you think that's a rather presumptuous request?"

"Well," I countered, "don't you believe God can give us a car?"

"Certainly He could. But maybe He wants us to be satisfied with what we have."

"I guess we'll see," I replied. "I've asked for it within three months."

"Three months?" he shouted. "I can't believe you."

One month passed. No sign of a car or extra money. I dug out my written contract. Feeling a little like Hezekiah when he spread out Sennacherib's letter before the Lord, I laid out mine.

"Lord," I prayed, "if I've made a mistake, I'll gladly withdraw it. Just let me know what I am supposed to do."

God didn't answer audibly. He simply gave me

bedrock assurance that I must continue believing. So I repeated my request, renewed my faith, and resumed trusting.

Two months passed. Still no sign of a car or extra money. We were barely squeaking through financially, and I knew unless a miracle occurred, there was no way anything, let alone a car, could materialize.

I went back to the Lord. Again, He urged me to trust Him. So again I recommitted my petition, thanked Him for the car, and bolstered up my dwindling confidence.

In January we drove from Colorado Springs to Dallas for the annual Texas Evangelism Conference. We visited dear friends in a church we had pastored twenty-two years previously. They insisted we return after the conference and spend another few days.

The conference ended January 15. We arrived the next day in Plainview, Texas to be with our friends.

That evening, January 16, a man from our old church appeared at our friends' door, came in and sat down.

"Harlan," he said immediately, "a group of your friends have collected some money, and we want to give you a new car."

"A new car!" my astonished husband exclaimed. He shook his head in unbelief. Then they took us out to view "God's car," and it was my turn to be astonished. There stood a shiny, beautiful new Mercury Marquis with every luxurious option known to the automobile industry.

When the full impact of the event hit us, we calculated and discovered that exactly three months to the day had passed since I hesitatingly signed my name to what seemed an impossible request.

Does God keep His promises? Does "anything" mean absolutely anything?

On January 16, 1981 I received proof.

Tom Illiff, a friend of ours, loves to say, "I know how to get anything I want—just want everything God wants for me."

The Power of Prayer

Jesus said, "Whatever you ask in my name, I will do." He didn't limit His offer to whether we are worthy, or have prayed enough, or witnessed enough. He gave us the power of His name—the almighty name of God's Son, His heir and the joint-heir of every believer. This means, of course, that everything Jesus possesses is ours, also.

When our son David was a student in a Texas seminary, he had a little circle of friends in his church who became his family away from home. I heard their names frequently, but we had not met them.

These friends planned a Colorado ski vacation, so without hesitation David invited them to stay at our house. He had not consulted us when he assured them, "My parents will be glad to have you."

When the friends appeared, it really didn't matter to us if it was convenient. David had confidence enough in his parents to believe we would honor any request he made for his friends. All they had to do was use our son's name, and everything we owned was available to them.

Jesus tells us, "You go to my Father. Tell Him I sent you, and He will give you everything you need."

Although the phrase *in the name of Jesus* is not a magic formula, it works much like a blank check. The prescribed amount is "all your need." It is like writing a letter listing every need and signing the name of Jesus at the end instead of your own name. Our praying releases Jesus so He can take over and go to work.

The Purpose of Prayer

"That the Father may be glorified in the Son," is the reason we pray. How can I be sure my request will bring glory to the Father? Two questions are helpful here:

1. Is my request in direct accordance with God's Word? (It is an indisputable law that God's will and God's Word always agree.)

2. Is my motive self-centered or God-centered?

For instance, when I am praying earnestly for a wayward child of mine to return to the Lord, do I need to agonize over whether it is God's will? Certainly not. It is never God's will for anyone to live in sin, so I can boldly pray for my child, knowing assuredly my Father will be glorified when that child is restored.

I learned this by personal experience. It was not until I fully grasped this truth and prayed confidently for a wayward child of mine that God brought her back to Himself. For years I had wavered. *Is it God's will?* I groped. *Can He change such a rebellious heart? Or has she sinned away her claim to God's grace?*

Stupid questions, I now see. When I dared to claim her for Christ, He turned that life around in less than a week — and she has never looked back. I often wonder if my vacillating faith imprisoned that girl longer than need be.

Learning How to Pray

"Jesus never mentioned unanswered prayer. He had the boundless certainty that prayer is always answered."[5]

Probably the best method to learn about prayer is to pray. We learn by doing — not by reading about it. The hours we spend reading books on prayer could probably be put to better use praying.

Begin by taking the Bible prayer promises you already know, and start exercising your faith by attaching those promises to specific areas of need in your life.

J. Sidlow Baxter is reported to have said, "Men may spurn our appeals, reject our message, oppose our arguments, despise our persons — but they are helpless against our prayers."

If this is true, my next question is a logical one. Why do we spend so much time complaining about our circumstances, conniving to escape them, and criticizing God and others for our misfortunes instead of doing the only thing that can change them: pray?

Oh, I know we all "say grace" before meals, mumble something at bedtime (blanket blessings), and a few of us even engage in a semblance of morning quiet time when it is convenient.

Yet almost every believer, when asked to pinpoint the weakest area in his Christian life, invariably answers, "lack of prayer." Many sincere ministers of the gospel confess the same.

How amazing is the phenomenon of prayerlessness when God has absolutely limited His people to this method as their only source of power. What possible reasons can we cite? Let's consider a few of them—some valid, some not.

We Do Have an Enemy

Have you ever noticed that when you determine to block out time for prayer, everything imaginable happens to thwart you? Ever wondered why?

For one thing, we have an enemy who is absolutely set upon making prayer impossible for us. Satan knows prayer is the powerhouse of the believer. It has been said that the devil fears nothing from our prayerless study, prayerless work, prayerless preaching . . . but he trembles when we kneel to pray.

Bill Bright, president of Campus Crusade for Christ, recalls that for more than a year before founding his worldwide organization, witnessing teams under his leadership regularly visited college dormitories, fraternities and sororities in the Los Angeles area.

"To my knowledge," he said, "not a single person committed his life to Christ at any of these meetings."

As soon as the Campus Crusade ministry was established in the spring of 1951, a twenty-four hour prayer chain was formed. Scores of Christians invested fifteen minutes every day in prayer for the new ministry.

"During the very first sorority meeting at UCLA after the prayer chain began," Bright said, "more than half of the sixty girls present expressed their desire to receive

Christ. In the next few months, over 250 students committed their lives to Jesus Christ."[6]

Is it any wonder Satan endeavors to thwart our prayer life? If he can't keep us from the daily act itself, when finally we get there, "the plague of flies begins"[7] — I must do this, I must do that. Make no mistake. Interruptions and wandering thoughts provide clear indication that our enemy is close at hand. If we give in and leave the prayer closet, he has won another victory. And who knows how many people suffer as a result of our prayerlessness?

Prayer Is Impractical

True intercession is spiritually draining. It doesn't make any sense in this achievement-oriented world to spend time accomplishing nothing. Besides, it is a thankless, unseen task. We love to preach, teach, sing, help others. But when we pray no one sees or applauds. Oswald Chambers writes that "Prayer is not practical, it is absurd; we have to realize that prayer is stupid from the ordinary common-sense point of view."[8]

One of the reasons we do not pray is that we are desperately trying to look sensible in the eyes of the world. So we "water down" the impracticalities of God's Word to make them mean something in accordance with common sense. If God's commands were only common sense, why should He bother?

We Are Too Busy

Prayer does not easily fit into busy schedules. To live in the 20th century is to encounter pressures and distractions which squeeze the very life from spiritual incentive.

Our busiest times, however, are when we most need to pray. Martin Luther realized this, so when he faced an extremely heavy day, he got up at 4 A.M. to be sure of sufficient time for prayer.

Sadly, those who are the busiest in Christian work

feel they cannot take time out to pray. We tend to substitute our over-energized activities for the prayer closet and wonder why people who seem ripe for the harvest never come to Christ. Simply reversing the order would allow our work to be done in less time, and we would find ourselves reaping a great harvest of souls. God works where we cannot.

It is true. There is no time in this busy life for prayer. The world takes no consideration for the quiet-time needs of God's people. If we pray, we will have to wrestle against the things that prevent us from getting to God.

We Don't Feel Like It

Hudson Taylor, whose life has been a shining inspiration to me, once said, "Sometimes when I pray, my heart feels like wood. But often the choicest answers come from those prayers."

All praying Christians can relate to the heart of wood. At those times we must force ourselves to shut the door deliberately on our emotions and pray without any feelings, if necessary.

Much of what I do every day falls into this category. I don't always feel like getting up in the morning. Or cooking. Or cleaning. Or writing. But positive results occur, whether I feel like it or not.

So I tell myself it really doesn't matter how I feel about prayer. The important thing is to do it. God doesn't trouble Himself with my feelings anyway. His only concern is that I obey.

The Bottom Line: Unbelief

Let's face the real culprit. We argue and try to explain away what God really meant when He said, "If you ask anything in my name, I will do it." We come up with all kinds of qualifying texts to prove that when He said *anything*, He didn't really mean it.

What we are actually saying is, "I don't believe

God." Just as soon as this kind of unbelief strikes, our prayer life is doomed. Faith flies out the window, and we begin to question God at every level.

The apostle James compares doubt in the heart of a believer to the waves of the ocean "blown and tossed by the wind." The conclusion he draws is enough to sober our minds. "That man (who doubts when he prays) should not think he will receive anything from the Lord; he is a double-minded man, unstable in all he does."[9]

So What Is the Solution?

Commit yourself. Make a daily appointment with the Lord. Set aside a specific time and place, and be as prompt with this appointment as with any other.

Keep a prayer diary. Record your requests and the date. Watch God work in supernatural ways.

Be specific with your requests. Generalization dulls the imagination and creates loss of incentive.

Visualize. Make mental pictures of the situations for which you are praying. See them as God sees them.

Pray blessings upon your enemies. Forgive everyone so your prayers will not be hindered.

Pray daily for our country's president and all those in authority "that we may lead a quiet and peaceable life."[10]

With such a weapon as prayer just a breath away, how can we ever excuse negligence or procrastination? Won't God hold each of us accountable for knowing to do good and refusing?

If we, by sacrificing a small portion of our day, can lift the load of our fellow believers, brighten their spirits and ours, and change our world—how can we afford to withhold this "cup of cold water" which our Father asks us to offer?

CHAPTER 8

Am I Qualified?

". . . the ultimate issue becomes not identity,
but meaning or purpose in life
based upon awareness of biblical self-identity."[1]

Why do some Christians move through life easily and with a high degree of success, while others stumble along barely able to hold together? This paradox exists even among family members who grow up in an identical environment.

A book title I recently heard captures my imagination: *Who We Are Is How We Pray.* I would like to suggest that who we *think* we are is how we *live.* Is it possible to be genetically endowed with strong bodies, superior abilities, and supreme intelligence—absolutely everything needed to succeed in life—and yet become a colossal failure? Yes, and not because potential is lacking, but simply because we *think* we can't succeed.

We Are Who We Think We Are

Several years ago we lived in Shelby, North Carolina during a time when "displaced persons" (politically oppressed people) came to the United States in large numbers. Many extremely well-educated and formerly prominent people from Latvia settled in our town.

Their plight was pathetic to me. They had fled the ruthless Soviet power machine just before it had taken over their beloved country. They came with little else than the clothes on their bodies. Citizens of Shelby had agreed to sponsor these people so they could at least have a place to stay during their painful transition.

Some of them were former writers, newspaper editors, and political leaders. Several had been renowned musicians in their country. All the members of "The Latvian Trio" came to our town.

I became especially well acquainted with a former concert pianist and his family. One day his wife told me in jeering fashion, "If my husband's mother could see him now, she would die of humiliation."

"Why?" I asked. "Since she stayed in Latvia, she must be in worse condition than he is."

"Oh, she is such a proud and haughty woman that nothing was ever good enough for her son — including me. His family was very wealthy, you see, and Valdemar was given anything he wanted. His mother always looked down on my family because we didn't fit into their social stratum."

I ignored her cynicism. "It must be especially difficult for Valdemar to be here with virtually nothing."

"You would think so, but I don't believe he even realizes he's poor," she replied indignantly. "He acts like he owns the whole world. I think people who grew up wealthy never seem to realize they are poor even when they have nothing. Look at him. He doesn't even own decent shoes, but he still thinks he's rich."

I've never forgotten my Latvian friend's observation. Whether she realized it or not, she expressed a classic gem of truth. We are who we think we are. This applies spiritually as well as in other realms. If we deeply believe what God says about who we are, our behavior will reflect that difference. We will then experience a drastic change from the former patterns of our defeated lifestyle.

Who Does God Say I Am?

Most people operate by memory. Memories of their

past, the family they were born into, their natural heredity, limitations of early childhood, traumatic experiences, deficiencies, lost opportunities, failures, and the like.

For instance, if a child while growing up is labeled "stupid" by family members, often in adulthood that person automatically assumes such a role. He may be brilliant, but the label sticks and prevents him from developing God-given potential.

Anorexics fall into this same category. I have counseled some of these women who appeared gaunt and looked like the pictures I've seen of Jewish holocaust victims. Yet their mental image of themselves is "fat." Nothing can dissuade them. They are killing themselves by food deprivation simply because they see themselves as needing to lose weight.

By such false measurements we determine our identity, both physically and spiritually. How the Father's heart must grieve over the lost potential of His redeemed children, especially when He has provided so adequately for us.

Who, indeed, are we? What resources have we been promised? Let's review briefly. As a believer, you are:

- An adopted child of God.
- God's heir and co-heir with His son, Jesus Christ. (This means that everything Jesus possesses is yours.)[2]
- A new person.[3]
- Dead to the old life, alive to the new.[4]
- More than a conqueror.[5]
- Possessor of all the strength you need.[6]
- Having all your needs supplied.[7]

The list could go on and on. Contained above, however, is enough evidence that God places a high value on the life of every single believer. All we need to do is believe Him whether we feel like it or not.

Let me make an important statement. The truest thing we can ever believe about ourselves is what God says of us. Doesn't it make sense that the one who created us is the only one capable of assessing our actual worth and identity? If that be so, in order to answer the age-old questions of "Who am I" and "Why am I here?" it is necessary to check with our authority: the Word of God.

We Are All Adopted

The concept of adoption gives us a picture of the true identity of each reborn child of God. We tend to lose sight of who we are in Christ through the daily grind of everyday living. And when this lofty concept is obscured, the spiritual struggle to live in overcoming power becomes more than we can handle.

The Bible says "in love He (God) predestined us to be adopted as sons (and daughters) through Jesus Christ..."[8] And it further declares that Jesus Christ came into this world "...that we might receive the adoption of sons (and daughters)."[9]

In the light of our glorious new status, we need to ponder two bewildering questions:

1. Why are believers so ignorant of this astounding truth that could set them free to be the persons God created them to be?

2. Why, when we actually know this fact, do we revert back to the limitations of our former identity and remain in bondage to the old life?

The Bible tells us that the reason we have received the indwelling Spirit of God is so that "we might *know* the things that are freely given to us of God."[10] Ignorance of these gifts, or neglect of them, keeps us constantly bound to the old life which can neither please God nor give us pleasure.

At the time of our adoption we received an entirely new identity. No longer are we bound to the old, natural life. God tells us we are brand new creations. "If anyone is in Christ, he is a new creation. The old has gone, the new has come!"[11] Never need we succumb to the old impoverished and imprisoned life that doomed us to certain failure.

What Determines The Kind Of Person I Become?

Our original thesis that it is one thing to know who we are in Christ but quite another to become that person, is now the focus of our attention. Frankly speaking, we have power through Jesus Christ to become all God created us to be. That the majority of believers never achieve the full status of God's original intention for their existence cannot be blamed upon any limitation on His part. We limit ourselves when we believe a lie about who we are.

Let's refer back to two examples already used. People often say, "I am stupid, therefore, I will always be an underachiever." Or, "I am fat. I won't look good unless I lose weight."

Many sincere Christians reason in the same way on a spiritual level. Having experienced past rejection or failure; they compare themselves with others and conclude they don't have the same opportunities and cannot be of much value in the kingdom of God. God goes to great lengths to tell us clearly who we are, why we are here, and what He wants to do with us.

We have only two choices. We can believe God, or we can forget His promises and move on with what we call "reality."

It is our prerogative to conclude that reality is what we see, feel, hear, and experience as opposed to the intangible qualities the Bible speaks about. In doing so, however, our unbelief nullifies the power God provided for us to live victoriously. One writer observes, ". . . victory is preceded by awareness of identity."[12]

Feelings or Facts?

Feelings have no valid bearing upon facts. As I write

this, it is January. At 6 o'clock in the morning when my alarm rings, it is still inky black outside, and it doesn't feel like morning to me. I look at my bedside clock in unbelief. It says 6:00, so whether I feel like it or not, the fact remains that it is morning. I can operate by feelings or facts, but my feelings do not change the fact that it is morning and time to crawl out of bed.

So if I am ever going to be the person God says I am, I must step out of the feelings realm and into the real world of fact. At first I don't feel like the person God says I am. But as I continue to live in the light of what He says about who I am, eventually I begin to feel like that person, and my Christian walk is transformed.

How Do I Change My Spiritual Self-Image?

Change does not take place overnight. It is a process, and we must come to terms with the fact that it will take time and persistence. For each of us the process will be slightly different. The following suggestions, however, will help bring about needful alterations if applied consistently.

1. Sincerely *ask God* to reveal through His Spirit the person He created you to be.

2. *Search the Scriptures* daily. In them you will discover who you are.

3. *Make a list* of verses and write down God's description. For example: "I am strong. I can do all things through Christ."[13] (Carry the list with you everywhere. Paste it on your mirror.)

4. *Begin to "act out the role."*

5. *Discard your feelings.* For instance, when you feel discouraged, search out a scriptural promise, focus on it alone, and completely disregard how you feel. A typical verse might be Joshua 1:9: "Be strong and very courageous. Do not be terrified; do not be discouraged, for the Lord your God will be with you wherever you go" (NIV).

6. *Speak in positive terms.* Do not express (or think)

negative statements about yourself, such as, "I'm just a weak person. I can't help it if I'm a failure."

7. By an act of your will, *replace the old mental image* of yourself with a visualization of the "new you" according to God's Word. Mentally image yourself living according to God's power.

No matter how you feel about your person or how poor a self-image you might possess, believe that you are precious in God's sight. If you are a child of God through faith in Jesus Christ, you can trust the one who said, "With man this is impossible, but with God all things are possible."[14]

"Is anything too hard for the Lord?"[15]

CHAPTER 9

The Decisive Factor

*"One individual life
may be of priceless value to God's purposes,
and yours may be that life."*[1]

During a period of my life when I was extremely busy with a number of important responsibilities, a visiting evangelist asked me a searching question.

"Madalene," he said, "are you completely sold out to Christ? Would you call yourself 100 percent faithful to Him?"

Now that's an incriminating question to ask a pastor's wife—which I was at that time. Did I dare speak the truth?

"Well, I'm really close," I finally said. "I don't think I could say 100 percent, but maybe ninety nine and nine-tenths percent." Then I smugly added, "I don't think anyone could say 100 percent and be honest, do you?"

Ignoring my question, he continued. "Supposing you told your husband you were ninety nine and nine-tenths percent faithful to him. Would he call you a faithful wife?"

His statement was like a glass of ice water thrown in my face. For years I had unconsciously played games with my commitment to Christ. Now, suddenly when compared to faithfulness in marriage, I could see the picture clearly enough to admit to myself that I was not 100 percent committed to Christ.

The truth was I had always held in reserve a minuscule percentage. Because I was so close to total commitment, and because it looked good on the outside, I deceived myself and others that I had, in fact, sold out. But it was that hair-breadth fraction of resistance that caused a lot of internal strivings which had already begun to surface externally. I could deceive others, but God knew my heart.

Now I understood the much-used cliché: "If He's not Lord of all, He's not Lord at all." I wasn't sure I liked it, either.

What Would I Do?

Now that my root problem was identified, I could no longer ignore it. God had put the issue to me squarely, and I had a choice.

To say I decided immediately to settle accounts and hand everything over to the Lord would be untrue. But I can say the visiting evangelist started me down a road that ultimately led to total commitment. Today I can state unequivocally that I am as faithful to the Lord as I am to my husband: 100 percent. But it didn't happen overnight. Or without difficulty.

When faced with the truth, I had to work through a number of disturbing possibilities. My time-consuming activities made me feel like an extremely important person. As a pastor's wife, I taught a large women's Bible study, sang in the choir, and made myself as available to members as time permitted. I still had one child in the home, so my mothering duties were not over. And I worked for an advertising agency writing business releases and feature stories for the local press.

Though I sincerely believed Jesus to be the focus of my life, what I didn't realize was that my true support system revolved around my activities. My ego thrived on the notion that I was a very needed person. I wasn't sure I could function without this attention. After all, I was just beginning to feel secure in an exciting identity, and I had carefully fitted all my activities into the "doing it for the Lord" mentality.

If I sold out completely to the Lord, what would happen to my cherished activities? My personal ambitions? My dreams?

1. Would the Lord force me to leave my prestigious position at the advertising agency?

2. Would He ask me to lay down my lifelong dream of being a writer?

3. Might He take one of my children?

4. Would He make us leave Colorado (which I loved) and send us to a less desirable field where I wouldn't be challenged?

5. Would He allow sickness to teach me lessons of patience? (Being well and strong was a big thing to me.)

Doesn't this sound absurd? Nevertheless, numbers of dreaded possibilities surfaced when I began to consider what might be involved if I surrendered myself completely to the Lord.

I finally had to admit that I was only a half-hearted follower of the Lord. One writer succinctly stated my dilemma: "There are plenty to follow our Lord half-way, but not the other half."[2] It took a long while for me to decide.

Total Commitment Defined

Now that I have taken the step which once appeared so frightening, I cannot imagine my former reservations. Compared to the benefits, resistance appears foolish—like a tearful child clutching an old, tattered toy while a loving father waits to replace it with a beautiful new one.

A simple working definition of total commitment is: *a once-and-for-all yielding of everything to God.* This involves a transfer of ownership. Since God takes better care of His belongings than we can, why not hand over to Him our lives and possessions?

Without question, we are living in a society which knows little of commitment at any level. Marriage and motherhood are prime examples. I remember clearly a time when I didn't know a single divorced couple. And for a mother to desert her children was almost more unthinkable than the possibility of God forsaking His. Today, both divorce and child desertion are so common as to surprise no one. A pledge, a vow, or a promise simply means "I will do this thing as long as it remains convenient."

Certainly this prevailing mindset affects every facet of our existence, and we unconsciously carry its crippling force into the church. So much so that earnest believers who sincerely seek to please God by yielding their lives to Him possess almost no concept of what it means or how to do it.

Partial Commitment

It's easy to say the right words, pray the right prayers, and conclude we have surrendered completely to God. The apostle Peter is a notable example.

"Even if I have to die with you, I will never disown you,"[3] he boldly declared to the Lord Jesus. Peter meant it. He sincerely thought he knew what he was saying.

The next recorded event is Gethsemane where Peter fell asleep after Jesus pleaded with him to stay awake during His agony. Following that scene we read of the three-fold denial which Jesus had predicted immediately after Peter's rash promise of undying loyalty. Peter didn't know his own heart. And neither do we.

After the birth of each of my four children, I sincerely gave them to the Lord. I really wanted these children to live for God's glory. For years I thought I had committed them unconditionally. Only when our oldest child rebelled during adolescence did I realize my commitment was conditional. Unknowingly, what I had really meant was, "Lord, I give you this child if she lives for your glory, if she won't disgrace me, if she stays well, if she doesn't die."

A similar example of conditional surrender occurred recently with a dear friend of ours. Cancer was diagnosed, and while he was going through the months of pre-surgery radiation treatments, he wrestled with his relationship with the Lord. At length he felt he had really sold out to the Lord, 100 percent.

"I am trusting the Lord completely," he told us with perfect sincerity. "Actually I have no choice, and I've come to realize it doesn't matter anyway. I just want God's will. If it's not His will to heal me, okay." With that statement, we rejoiced that he had finally reached the point of absolute surrender.

Only surgery revealed what no one, including himself, knew: that his commitment was conditional. His subsequent anger and depression revealed his true spirit when the surgeon disclosed that he couldn't possibly eradicate all the cancer.

It became evident that what our friend really meant was, "Lord, I surrender myself to you if the surgery is successful, if all the cancer is removed, and if I live." Please don't misunderstand. I'm not saying this kind of commitment is easy. Because we are so easily deceived, our commitment must be tested. Only the Lord knows the truth of what lies buried within our hearts. So much rubbish obscures the genuine that even we can't sort through it. It takes an all-knowing, all-seeing, objective eye to expose our true intent.

So if we ever reach the place where Jesus Christ is Lord of all, we must submit to God's scrutiny. For a long time all I could say was, "Lord, I want to be fully surrendered. I don't know how, but I give you permission to do in my life whatever is necessary to bring me to that point."

Such a prayer is frightening. I tried to imagine what God might be forced to do in answer to my prayer — either to me or to someone I loved. But eventually I learned that

God is faithful when He says, "Ask, and you shall receive, that your joy may be full."[4]

Total Commitment—The Only Way

Before considering the "how" of surrender, let's look at a masterful illustration of "who" and "what" it is. The apostle Paul in his letter to the Philippian church gives enticing insight: ". . . To me to live is Christ, to die is gain".[5] Total commitment enabled Paul to give up his right to his own life.

This verse embodies a specific decision—to surrender unconditionally everything we are, everything we have, and everything we ever expect to be or have.

My first experience wrestling with such a choice came during my freshman year at Wheaton College. Every Tuesday night my little circle of friends attended the FMF (Foreign Mission Fellowship) prayer meeting on campus. It was important for me to be with them, not necessarily to be at the FMF meeting. So I went. Certainly I had no interest in foreign missions.

Before long I found myself confronted with what I perceived to be a call from God to surrender to foreign missions. For two months I resisted. I lived those months in absolute agony.

Why didn't I immediately say, "Of course, Lord! There is nothing I'd rather do than serve You wherever You want me"?

Simple. In my mind God was saying, "Madalene, I want you to spend the rest of your days in Africa."

What? Bury myself in the darkest of jungles? Not on your life!

Two months later, dog-tired and sick of the struggle, I whispered faintly, "All right, Lord. If that's what You want, I'll do it."

Instantly, and I mean the moment the words left my mouth, the tension left me. It was as if the Lord was saying, "I don't want you in Africa. I only wanted your willingness to go."

Had I not fought through to an affirmative reply, might I still be floundering as to what God's will is for my life? I honestly wonder.

Paul's total commitment transferred confidence from his own abilities to Christ's.

Paul's "profit and loss statement" appears in Philippians 3. It didn't hurt his pride to say that all the things he formerly considered profitable, he now considered loss for the sake of Christ.

He also said, "I can do all things through Christ who strengthens me."[6] So he didn't have to muster ability on his own to accomplish the tasks God had called him to do. Enablement beyond his limited strength became available.

Why does the work of the Lord move so slowly? Why are we so often bogged down trying to do the things God has called us to do? For the most part, both church and believer attempt to accomplish God's calling with human ability. And it doesn't work.

Total commitment fixed Paul's focus completely on Christ.

"That I may know Him, and the power of His resurrection, and the fellowship of His sufferings . . ."[7] became Paul's absolute passion. His goal wasn't that he be a better servant of Christ's, or that he be a more effective evangelist or even win more souls to Christ. Jesus Christ Himself became the all-consuming purpose for which Paul existed.

Therefore he was not constantly sidetracked, running up and down dead-end streets searching for his life's destiny. That issue was settled forever when he made Jesus Christ absolute Lord of his life.

Greatness in God's Eyes

We Christians often have a twisted understanding of what pleases God. We become exhausted racing to Bible studies, conferences and retreats trying to learn more about the Bible. The trouble is, our brains are already bursting with knowledge we have no time to apply.

A humorous example of this happened to me on a cold, icy day last winter. On this day, my car engine died. I brought my car to a stop adjacent to another car parked in front of a private residence, then I sent up a quick prayer: "Lord, please send someone to help me."

Just at that moment a lady walked out of the house carrying a baking dish covered with aluminum foil. She opened the door of the car next to mine. *There's my answer!* I immediately thought.

I stepped out and asked if she would be so kind as to give my battery a quick boost because my car wouldn't start.

"Oh, I'm sorry," she said. "I don't have time."

"I have cables," I assured her.

"But I'll be late for my church supper."

"Honestly," I pleaded, "it won't take three minutes, and I would be so grateful if you could do it."

Ever so reluctantly, she consented. It took only two minutes, and I don't think she was late for her church function.

As I drove away I thought, what is this church business all about anyway? Are we so hung up on trivialities (like not being seconds late for a meeting) that we can ignore people along the way who need help?

No wonder the world criticizes Christians. No wonder they sneer at us and refuse to come near our beautifully decorated monuments to hypocrisy. That's all our churches and our Christianity represent to many of them.

When are we ever going to discover what Jesus really came to teach us? "For to me to live is *Christ!*" Paul didn't say "for to me to live is cramming my head full of doctrine, always being on time, winning the perfect attendance award, owning the Bible with the most verses underlined, or teaching the largest Bible class."

"I tell you," Jesus said, "unless you change and become like little children, you will never enter the kingdom of heaven . . . whoever humbles himself like this child is the greatest in the kingdom of heaven."[8]

Counting The Cost

I submit to you that the act of total commitment is a humbling process. That's why so many believers never make it. Let's move a step further. That is why so many lack even the desire for the Christ-surrendered life. We tenaciously cling to those cheap substitutes that pump us up to an inflated sense of our own importance.

The objections I felt when the evangelist confronted me about my spiritual commitment now seem unthinkable. But what are your objections? The first step might be to write down the reasons you are afraid to surrender your life to Jesus.

Do you fear that your popularity might dwindle? Or you will miss business opportunities and financial prosperity? Or you would be forced to give up some questionable pleasure? Or friends?

Formulas are cheap and easy to devise. The cost of pursuing Christ alone is high, make no mistake. But the cost of refusal is eternally higher.

Benjamin Franklin wrote a humorous essay entitled "The Whistle." He tells of an incident that took place when he was a child of seven. His family and friends filled his little pocket with coins on a holiday, so he trotted off to the toy store.

After inspecting all the trinkets, he chose a shiny whistle and piled all of his coins on the counter in exchange. His trip home was delightful. He blew the whistle over and over, and the shrill tone enchanted him.

When he arrived home, his brothers and sisters and friends all laughed and made fun of him because he had paid too much for the cheap, tin whistle. Suddenly his pleasure turned to despair, and he hated the whistle.

But he learned a valuable lesson which lasted an entire lifetime. Whenever he faced a crucial decision, these words came to him:

"Don't pay too much for your whistle."

We make these decisions every day. We can buy the whistles—the cheap, useless objects bringing only temporary joy. We can invest every minute of our lives pursuing material things, status symbols, peer acceptance. But we will always pay too much.

Having been on both sides of the fence, I want to say emphatically that no reason, however justified at the time, is worth sacrificing the exciting possibilities for which God created us.

Jesus calls us to forsake all and follow Him. He did not say it would be easy. He only said it would be worth it.

CHAPTER 10

Delivered From Powerlessness

*"The Holy Spirit cannot be located
as a guest in a house.
He invades everything."*[1]

My husband has an old Jeep—and I do mean old. He's had her so long he can't bear to part with the beloved relic. Our neighbor has affectionately dubbed her "Old Yaller" because she is mostly yellow.

Old Yaller is kept only for hauling logs, plowing snow in winter, and doing tough, mountain jobs. My husband doesn't care if he slides into a tree and dents her. He merely pounds out the dent and buys a can of spray paint. She doesn't look great with several shades of yellow, but she never goes down the mountain anyway.

Old Yaller had not been acting right last summer. Nevertheless, we took a group of visitors up a steep series of mountain ranges in the Roosevelt National Forest boundering our community. We wanted them to see a breathtaking view of rock formations dubbed "Gog and Magog."

Our only problem was that Old Yaller gave out before we got there, and everyone had to walk quite a distance. We became so weary that we hardly enjoyed the magnificent scenery. Our six-year-old granddaughter, recounting the event to her mother, said, "Mom, I got so thirsty I nearly croaked."

The next time we made the trip we drove an almost new four-wheel-drive Bronco. The motor purred and hummed, and its power made those steep ascents seem like a California freeway. We didn't even think about the possibility of a breakdown on that day. Spellbound by the scenery, we stopped at beautiful overlooks, picked flowers, drank from a cool mountain stream and thoroughly enjoyed the trip.

What made the difference? The margin of power.

This story illustrates the contrast between Christians who are struggling with all their might to make the Christian life operate, and those who live and work and walk and talk in the power of the Holy Spirit.

The Grim Determination Society

We often find ourselves earnestly praying with the psalmist, "May the words of my mouth and the meditations of my heart be pleasing in your sight, O Lord . . ."[2] Then we set out to accomplish this goal ourselves.

"Tomorrow I'm going to be spiritual," we say. "Today I talked too much. I criticized too much. But tomorrow I'm not going to do it. I am determined to please God."

What happens tomorrow? The same things that happened today. Why? Because it is impossible to overcome fleshly tendencies by human effort and determination.

I have a friend who constantly battles overweight and overeating. She has failed at every diet she ever attempted, and there have been "thousands." Finally she admitted, "I hate the word diet, and if I have the feeling I am restricted and can't eat when I'm hungry, something inside me goes crazy. No matter how badly I want to lose weight, I find myself eating what I shouldn't."

". . . I have the desire to do good," Paul said, "but I cannot carry it out."[3] In other words, I know *what* to do, but I don't *how* to do it.

Our spiritual problem is that we are trying to do the

work of the Spirit of God in the energy of the flesh. That's why Christians (and churches) are so powerless today.

The only way to sustain continual victory in our lives is to live and walk in the Spirit of God. The trouble is, we run back and forth between flesh and Spirit, and then we wonder why we are constantly defeated. We become needlessly confined in the prison of our fleshly energies and never discover the glorious freedom of soaring in God's Spirit.

Imprisoned by Ignorance

A few years ago I heard a man on the Phil Donahue Show tell a story from his childhood. He told of seven baby ducks who were put into a pen one day on his family's iso-lated farm. It was a simple enclosure constructed of lightweight chicken wire. The ducks stayed in the pen and grew to maturity. Although the top remained open, they never flew out—not because they were unable, but because they just thought they couldn't.

One day someone inadvertently left the door open. Out they waddled. Immediately two big dogs tore them to pieces. They could have flown out of danger, but they didn't think they could.

Alas, they lived needlessly confined all their lives, and finally they died prematurely.

We are like those ducks. Something is tragically missing from our day-to-day experience. We have wings, but we don't know how to use them. We are unable to rise into the freedom of God's Spirit as He intended.

The truth is, we don't even know we have wings be-cause we are afraid to allow God to take full control of our lives. We harbor a twisted, warped idea that if we surrender fully to God, He will take away everything we love and force us to do the things we don't want to do. How preposterous!

"If you then, though you are evil, know how to give good gifts to your children, how much more will your Father in heaven give good gifts to those who ask Him."[4]

What Is the Spirit-Filled Life?

The first appearance on this earth of the Holy Spirit came at Pentecost and is described in Acts 2. Jesus had been taken up bodily into heaven by the Father. His followers watched helplessly as their crucified, resurrected leader vanished from their sight. Before He left, however, Jesus promised to send His Spirit. Not knowing exactly what to expect, 120 of these bewildered disciples waited alone in a large room for ten days.

Suddenly this promised Presence filled both the room and each of Jesus' followers who were gathered and waiting. Those who had been fearful and uncertain before Pentecost now arose with great boldness and strength. No one could intimidate them ever again. They were filled with a new source of power — the same power that is available to every believer from Pentecost to this moment.

Frankly, I am sick of hearing people use the term "Spirit-filled" when they haven't the foggiest notion what it's all about. What they usually mean is church members who appear to be superspiritual. They may be rigorously faithful to church, teach Sunday school, participate regularly in the visitation program.

Hannah Whitall Smith observes that, "Apparent zeal for the truth may hide a spirit of criticism, or intellectual pride. Apparent Christian faithfulness may hide an absence of Christian love. Apparent thrift and prudence in the management of our affairs may hide a lack of trust in God."[5] Therefore, it is impossible to judge by appearances who is filled with the Holy Spirit and who is not.

Let's make clear the sometimes controversial point about when one actually receives the Holy Spirit. It happens at the time of conversion. At that moment we receive all of the Holy Spirit because the Holy Spirit is a person, and it is impossible to receive only part of a person.

The critical issue, however, is that the Holy Spirit does not receive all of us at that time. Ideally, this is what should happen. But for most of us it does not. "As long as we are rich," Oswald Chambers wrote, "possessed of anything in the way of pride or independence, God cannot do anything for us. It is only when we get hungry spiritually that we receive the Holy Spirit."[6]

To be Spirit-filled cannot be described as a high plateau reached only after arduous discipline and self-abasement. If that were so, fleshly effort would be the route. Paul refuted such a notion when he wrote to the Galatian believers, "Are you so foolish? Having begun by the Spirit, are you now being perfected by the flesh?"[7]

It is my earnest conviction that being filled with the Spirit is "a truth to be believed, and an experience to be received."[8] It doesn't matter what you call it, let's not get bogged down in semantics. Godly men have used various terminology to describe the experience. Among them are:

- Spirit-filled life
- Exchanged life
- Spirit baptized life
- Abundant life
- Life that wins
- Second work of grace

I heard a preacher once say that "it doesn't matter how high you jumped when it happened, but how straight you walked afterwards."[9] So the evidence of the Spirit-filled life is obedience.

Until we have obeyed what we already know, God never reveals more truth about Himself. That's why few of us ever enter into the glorious reality of the Spirit-filled life. We refuse to abandon ourselves wholly to God and pay the price He demands.

What The Spirit-filled Life Is Not

Often I hear people say, "I want to be baptized in the Holy Spirit." To be sure, that is a noble and worthy desire—the highest of all spiritual goals. I do wonder, however, what they actually mean.

Are they saying, "I'm tired of this constant battle with the flesh and daily problems, and I want it to stop"? In other words, do they want life to be easier? More fun? I wish someone would show me in the Bible where it says the Christian life is easy or fun. I've never found it.

Sometimes I think Christians look at what may be termed the glamour of the Spirit-filled life. They are like Simon the sorcerer, who wanted it so badly he tried to pay the apostles for the power he saw them exercise.[10] These people are captivated by the supernatural, and they genuinely desire what they see.

There is nothing wrong with that, except usually they are seeking the fruit without the process of producing it. Despair sets in when they cannot attain this objective. But they have missed the point of the Spirit-filled life.

The sole purpose of the Holy Spirit in our lives is, in the words of Oswald Chambers, to "expound the nature of Jesus to me in order to make me one with my Lord, not that I might go off as a showroom exhibit."[11] The apostle Paul stated God's purpose clearly when he said, "I have been crucified with Christ, and it is no longer I who live, but Christ lives in me . . ."[12]

God did not send His Spirit to make life easier, or to enable us to put up a better front before a perishing world. He sent His Spirit to fill us with Jesus, His beloved Son, and to empower us to do the work Jesus began in this world. "You shall receive power . . . and you shall be My witnesses . . ."[13]

To fill a container with one substance, clearly it must be emptied of all other substances. It is a contradiction of terms to speak of being filled with God's Holy Spirit and yet be motivated by self-centered, self-fulfilling, personal ambitions. Either it is one or the other.

How, Then, Can We Be Filled?

The Spirit-filled life is costly. It cost the Savior His

precious life blood, and it will cost us everything we own. That's why so few ever find it — they think the price is too high. But Paul said, "I count all things but loss for the excellency of the knowledge of Christ Jesus my Lord; for whom I have suffered the loss of all things . . ."[14] He wasn't grieving over his loss; he compared it all to mere rubbish when measured with the joy of being Spirit-filled.

That's exactly what all the things are that we keep clinging to — rubbish. Hindrances. After we lay them down, we understand what Paul meant. Suddenly our vision becomes clear, our lives are free from former obstacles, and we are liberated to fulfill God's highest purposes. But we don't know this until after we have paid the price.

I believe there are five essential steps to being filled with God's Spirit of power and holiness. They are:

1. Deal conclusively with sin in your life.

This first step is the one we struggle to avoid at all costs. All our lives we have endeavored to push the pain of sin and its consequences out of sight. Most of our confessions have been made to relieve the discomfort sin brings and to cram it into some hidden crevice where it won't bother us any longer. Or we do it to escape consequences. Such confessions cannot be construed as having dealt conclusively with sin.

A dear, elderly veteran missionary to China, "Miss Bertha" Smith, insists that if anyone really wants to be filled with the Holy Spirit, he/she must make a sin list. To do this, she instructs, simply get a yellow lined pad, ask God to reveal every unconfessed sin in your life, and write it down. It may take a week, it may take a month. But do not stop until you know it is complete.

One of my sons took to heart what Miss Bertha said at a Bible conference. For many days afterward he carried a little pad everywhere. His wife recalled that often during the middle of the night she would be conscious of the bedside lamp being snapped on, a momentary scribbling, and the light being quickly switched off. Although it may appear a dismal prospect to focus so intently upon past sin, it is necessary if we are to walk in freedom. Satan gains access into our lives through unresolved sin.

The mountain community in Colorado where we live, Crystal Park, contains slightly more than 2,000 acres. It is a private membership association with a single road and electronically controlled gate accessing the entire acreage. The gate provides welcome protection to all our residents from outside harm.

Except that a privately owned tract of eighty acres borders at the top edge of Crystal Park. A family living in eastern United States has owned this tract for three generations. We have no choice but to allow them access through our gate and up our road. Living at such a distance, however, they seldom visit.

Now they want to subdivide and sell their property. Our closed community could be open to all sorts of unwelcome and dangerous intrusion. That eighty acres hidden away at the top of the mountain might be the means of allowing total access to strangers, and we can do nothing about it unless we buy the property.

Sin in our lives is like that eighty acres. As long as Satan controls even the smallest fragment, he has access to his property. Like it or not, we can't keep him out. And with eighty acres belonging to him, or even one, we cannot ever be filled with God's Spirit. "Let us lay aside every encumbrance, and the sin which so easily entangles us . . ."[15]

Miss Bertha says when the sin list is complete, thoroughly repent and confess each one before God. Until we fully realize He is the One Who has been wronged, we will never experience true repentance. With every sin we commit, we are pounding another spike into Jesus' body and saying, Take that! Take that!

David thoroughly understood this. Although he murdered a man and committed adultery with the man's wife, he cried to God, "Against you, you only have I sinned and done what is evil in your sight . . ."[16]

After repentance and confession, take a match and burn the list. Watch the flames destroy the evidence. Then when the enemy stalks up to accuse you, all you have to do is point to Jesus and the fact that He has forgiven you for those sins.

The next step is almost as difficult:

2. *Surrender unconditionally everything you are and everything you have.*

Lay it all down forever. This involves a decisive act of the will. Watchman Nee said, "Not all who preach consecration are consecrated people. Not all who understand the doctrine of consecration know the reality of consecration."[17]

Nee speaks of the necessity of building an altar in our lives just as Abraham built an altar. "This altar was not for sin offering, but for burnt offering. It was not a matter of settling the sin question, but of offering the life to God."[18]

With the sin question already settled in step one, now we must offer ourselves. "I beseech you therefore, brethren, by the mercies of God, to present your bodies a living sacrifice, holy, acceptable to God . . ."[19] Be certain you withhold nothing. Picture an altar in your mind, and place treasured objects, beloved family members and friends along with your own body upon it.

At the time God was dealing with me on this point, I walked around our house viewing everything in it. Mentally I placed each object on the altar. Certain things grasped at my heart like a magnet making it more difficult. But I persisted until I could release them and come to the place of surrendering everything to God for His disposal. If He wanted to remove anything from me, that was His business. If not, that was His business also.

"There was a day when I died, utterly died," said George Mueller. "I died to George Mueller, his opinions, preferences, tastes, and will—died to the world, its approval or censure—died to the approval or blame even of my brethren and friends . . ."[20]

3. Ask God to fill you with the Holy Spirit.

"If you then, though you are evil, know how to give good gifts to your children, how much more will your Father in heaven give the Holy Spirit to those who ask him."[21]

4. Believe that He has filled you.

No matter what you feel, or don't feel, believe that the transaction is completed. Do not become obsessed with signs at this point. You may experience great emotions, visible evidence, or none. We are not told to seek signs. The fullness of the Holy Spirit will be confirmed with a renewed love for the Savior, a passion for God's Word, and a power to accomplish God's purposes for your life.

In my own experience, after I had asked God to fill me with His Holy Spirit, I was conscious of an absolute inner calmness replacing a former spirit of constant anxiety. I couldn't remember a time in my life previously when I did not feel inwardly tense. Suddenly the tension was all drawn out of me. God had met me at the point of my most crucial need.

The fifth step is extremely important.

5. Give God permission to go to work.

Our human tendency is to help God effect change in our lives. The truth is we haven't been able to change ourselves during all the previous years of our life. So why not give God a chance? He can. But He needs our permission to do whatever is necessary in order to transform us into the image He originally designed for us.

Revival Could Come

If God's people in America really meant business in their Christian lives and allowed the Holy Spirit to fill them constantly, I believe we would see worldwide revival in no time at all. The gospel we preach is not believable to the lost world around us because of the lack of verification in our lives.

Mahatma Ghandi is reported to have said that he was greatly attracted to Jesus Christ, but he could not become a Christian because the followers of Jesus were so little like Him.

Might this discrepancy be verified by our constant wrangling over the fine points of interpretation about the doctrine of the Holy Spirit instead of letting Him go ahead and fill us? If so, let's stop the wrangling and get on with the work of God.

PART THREE

Finally Arriving!

At last the mountain is conquered! Persistence has won out, and with the intense climbing behind, a glowing sense of satisfaction replaces the former exertion. The weary traveler is now able to rest beside a refreshing stream and savor the peacefulness of the surrounding beauty.

CHAPTER 11

Freedom at Last!

Contentment is not getting what I want,
but wanting what I get.

True contentment is the quest of a lifetime. A few achieve it. More do not. Our basic human nature is one of restlessness, always seeking more worlds to conquer, never being satisfied.

A newspaper cartoon illustrates these basic tendencies. Pictured were two fields divided by a fence. Both fields were the same size, and each had plenty of the same kind of green, lush grass.

In each field there was a single mule, and each mule had his neck stretched through the fence eating grass from the other mule's pasture. In the process, the mules caught their heads between fence wires and were unable to extricate themselves.

The artist wrote a single word caption at the bottom of the picture: *Discontent.*[1]

Humorous? Yes. At the same time it is sad to consider the human counterpart with its wasted lives and years pursuing the myth of the greener pasture.

The earmark of our society in this 20th century is the absence of contentment. We have been correctly labeled the "now" generation. Unable to wait for anything, we demand instant gratification for our whims and instant relief from the slightest discomfort.

Many of us were not born during this particular

generation, yet its deadly philosophy has slipped into our subconscious as well. The current drug explosion, our staggering national debt, the moral collapse of our nation with its accompanying epidemic of social diseases, divorce—all have their roots in discontent. Christians are not exempt from the gnawing discontent of our age even though they should be.

Where Does It All Start?

While the greener pasture syndrome embodies an inner spirit of discontent, external factors feed the infection and keep the disease flourishing. We may blame our malady on economic pressures beyond our control, but that is merely a pretext.

Let's look at a few widespread practices that keep the virus of discontent alive and tempt us to plunge into debt far beyond our ability to survive.

- The availability of credit cards—buy now, pay later.
- Alluring advertisements and commercials of the media.
- The emphasis on "nothing down, small monthly payments."
- Television depiction of an affluent lifestyle as typical of all American families.
- Banks and finance companies that encourage a process of continual refinancing to consolidate all debts.
- The newest gimmick—no down payment, no carrying charges.

While I was teaching a recent series on "A Scriptural Plan for Financial Freedom," one of the men in the class placed a cartoon on my podium. A buyer was sitting at the desk of a loan officer and signing a purchase contract.

"How many years of payments are there?" he asked.

"All of them," was the unflinching answer.

How innocently we seem to fall into the monthly payment trap before we realize the awful truth — we never dig out. As Richard Foster writes, "Contemporary culture is plagued by the passion to possess. The unreasoned boast abounds that the good life is found in accumulation, that 'more is better.' "[2]

I am constantly amazed at the financial catastrophes typical of most American families. Christians. Young couples. Many of the stresses tearing marriages apart today relate directly to financial mismanagement, a result of discontent.

A young couple in my Bible class came to me not long ago.

"Would you please go over our financial situation with us?" they asked. "We don't know what to do. Linda wants to stay home with our two babies, but it looks as if she will be forced to go back to work."

We spread out all the papers listing their income, current expenses, bills, and each debt. When I discovered this young couple in their mid-twenties was already $30,000 in debt, I couldn't believe it. They cited valid reasons (to them) for each obligation.

"Nothing but a miracle straight from God can help you," I told them after lengthy dialogue and consideration. "In the meantime, let's try to understand why you are so hopelessly in debt."

The problem turned out to be compulsive spending on the part of the young husband. Interestingly, this couple (and most I have counseled) never stop to consider the overall price of a purchase — only the monthly payment and whether they can afford that amount. Carrying charges may push the price to double or more, but it seems not to matter. When emergencies develop, there are no reserve funds to prevent plunging deeper into the bottomless pit.

Don Osgood compares this situation to "The little snowball at the top of the hill [that] has become a smothering giant as it rolls down the hill towards us. That's the stressful predicament we get into with family finances."[3]

The most disheartening aspect of this pattern is that every facet of our lives becomes infected — spiritually as well as materially. While the beginning of our woes may be spawned in the financial area, grasping tentacles spread everywhere. A description of most American families can be found in the following:

- We never have enough of anything, including money.
- We are miserable in our homes and families because nobody measures up to TV standards.
- We are unhappy in our churches.
- Our work brings no satisfaction because conditions aren't ideal.
- We drive ourselves and our families crazy as we run around trying to fill the void.
- We're always searching, searching, searching and never experiencing deep-down, inner contentment.

When Christians find themselves locked into such a lifestyle, what kind of message are we sending out to the lost world around us? More specifically, what kind of children are we thrusting into that world?

Can This Be God's Will?

When confronted with scriptural directives in the matter of debt or the need to be content, I hear a great deal of rationalization.

"We're not living in Bible times. It's different now."

"It's a tough world out there. Nobody is making it these days."

"When our parents were young, it was easier to buy houses, save money, make ends meet."

"Things cost a lot more. You can't compare today's standards with any other."

While all of the above may be true, God's unchanging Word still stands, and it says, "Be content with such things as you have, for He [God] has said, I will never leave you nor forsake you."[4]

And Paul could say, "I have learned in whatsoever state I am therewith to be content."[5]

When Paul wrote those words, circumstances were far from ideal for him. The fact is, he was in prison. This could not have been a desired circumstance. Certainly it was an unwelcome interruption to crucial ministry. Wouldn't his confinement hinder God's purposes?

What Paul realized is something we fail to grasp. If God is sovereign, He is in control of our circumstances. What may appear to be a disaster could be the precise situation needed to bring about God's perfect will in our lives. That was why Paul could speak not only of contentment, but of great joy and rejoicing in Christ even while in prison.

So a liberating principle can be drawn here. And it's all wrapped up in a mysterious phrase that the apostle Paul especially loved.

"In Christ" Is the Key

The first time I fully realized the meaning of this concept, we lived and pastored in North Carolina. When we arrived there, our first baby was three months old. We were practically bride and groom. Seven years later, when we left, we carried three children with us. The memories of those wonderful years still remain.

Though we were young and inexperienced, the people loved us and treated us as their own children. It was natural that they were sad when God called us to another field.

"How can you trade this beautiful country for the windswept prairies of Texas?" everyone asked.

That is when I understood that as long as I am abiding "in" Christ, it doesn't matter where my body is "at"—North Carolina, Texas, Africa. My true abiding place, my true location, does not change.

Contentment: A Learned Response

If Paul could be content in prison, can we possibly be content with all we possess by comparison? Most assuredly, yes. God never tells us to do anything impossible for us to achieve

A quick review of some of the principles enabling Paul to learn contentment will be helpful here.

"Don't worry about anything..."[6]

Notice there is no qualifier in this command. It doesn't say "Don't worry except, or only, or if." It just says *don't* worry about anything. This means big issues, little ones, and those in-between.

Vance Havner once said, "Worry is like a rocking chair. It will give you something to do, but it won't get you anywhere."[7]

"In everything give thanks..."[8]

When we learn to be thankful for everything, we move a long way down the road to contentment. It's easy to be thankful for the good things that come into our lives, but the real test is thanking God for the things that don't appear good.

Begin now by making a list of all the negative circumstances in your life. One by one, thank God for each—whether you feel like it or not. Feelings have nothing to do with obeying God. Tell Him you are doing it purely out of obedience.

You will be amazed how quickly your whole attitude changes when you adopt a thankful spirit.

Suffering is a part of living.

No one is exempt. Paul was grateful that God had counted him worthy to suffer for Christ's sake. His supreme goal, he said, was "That I may know Him [Christ] . . . and the fellowship of His sufferings . . ."[9]

Few Americans in comparison to the rest of the

world know much about suffering, especially in the area of economic hardship. We are beginning to learn because of our foolish spending practices.

Perhaps a little suffering of material need will turn to our ultimate blessing so that we can acquire a more realistic view of the stewardship of our resources. Elizabeth Elliott says that "It usually takes loss or deprivation in some measure for most of us to count the blessings we so readily take for granted."[10]

Paul wrote, "For unto you it is given in the behalf of Christ, not only to believe in Him, but also to suffer for His sake." And, "If we suffer, we shall also reign with him."[11]

How Can We Learn Contentment?

Without considering practical methods of dealing with the chaos of our finances, we can never learn contentment.

George Mueller of Bristol, England declared that the first thing to do is confess the sin of debt. Until we fully realize debt is sin, we cannot attain a spirit of contentment.

Mueller cites the second step to be confession of another sin—that of not tithing. When money is scarce, it's easy to believe we cannot afford to tithe. But the real question is, can we afford *not* to tithe? Even the most superficial reading of Malachi 3 is convincing.

Following these two confessions, I would like to add six proven suggestions for reversing a financially crippling lifestyle. My husband and I personally practice all of them:

1. Learn to live within your means. Buy nothing, absolutely nothing, for which you cannot pay. It is no disgrace to do without what you cannot afford.

2. Destroy your credit cards. Yes, *every* last one of them. It is infinitely easier to fall into the trap when you don't have to pay cash.

3. Begin saving ahead for items you need. Enormous amounts of money are gained by not paying interest

or carrying charges.

4. Purchase nothing under compulsion. Compulsive spending is one of the worst enemies of contentment and keeps more families deeply in debt than almost anything else.

5. Determine by prayer and revelation the standard of living God desires for you. When that is attained, place anything left over at God's disposal.

6. "Owe no man anything but to love." Stay out of debt!

Contentment Demands a Changed Lifestyle

Most of these principles are self-evident. Number five may cause a bit of consternation because of the widespread American practice of spending every available dollar to continually upgrade the standard of living.

Japanese people, it is reported, save 17 percent of their income, while Americans save less than 3 percent. As a result, Japan controls four out of the five largest banking institutions in the world, which explains why their economy is booming and ours is staggering under an ever-increasing load of debt. The money (with its obvious interest-bearing power) saved by the private sector in Japan is deposited in their banks making it available for expansion, while we are forced to borrow for our economy.

This philosophy works for (or against) individuals as well as nations. "Deficit spending will work no better for you than it does for the federal government," writes Richard Foster in *Freedom of Simplicity*.[12] If we spend all we earn simply to upgrade our standard of living, a vicious cycle is initiated: Spending, instead of saving, becomes a habit.

This, in turn, keeps our focus on the constant acquisition of material possessions. Our money, then, is tied up in the never-ending process of monthly payments so that nothing is available to the Lord. We are then convinced we can't afford to tithe, to be generous, or to save.

Ultimately, our standard of living becomes so escalated that we are forced to be dollar conscious in order to support a foolishly luxurious lifestyle.

Today in our sagging economy, we see the folly of this behavior everywhere. Bankruptcy rates are skyrocketing. Businesses are failing almost daily. Unprecedented numbers of people, we are told, find no place to live but in the streets.

Even churches are caught up in this never-ending treadmill. Numbers of them we personally know about are so debt-ridden through overbuilding that they can barely meet mortgage payments. Some are even returning to the old edifices they abandoned in order to cut expenses to a more realistic position.

A church in Oklahoma is one case in point. The former pastor built up a huge congregation. This was the leading church for many years among Southern Baptists in baptisms and attendance. A spirit of excitement charged the atmosphere every Sunday.

Rather than increase the number of services and remain in the old building, the church relocated and built an elaborate 7,000 seat auditorium. Attendance dropped off, giving decreased, and the mortgage payments have all but wiped out funds to do the work God called the church to accomplish.

If Christians alone would stop living by the false standards of the world and begin tithing and saving, not only would our personal financial problems be solved, but our national economy would begin to reverse itself. God's Word is still the best and only guide for His people.

"The Proof of the Pudding"

Recently I received a letter from a pastor's wife. My husband and I had taught a five-day series of meetings in her husband's church. We included a team presentation on the subject of "The Joy Of Contentment."

A large number of people in attendance made a com-

mitment to give at least a six-month trial to the above principles. The pastor and his wife were among those most
deeply convicted.

"The Lord is so good to us," she writes. "We
destroyed all our credit cards after you left, and we knew
we would be forced to trust Him for everything.

"Well, Graham [her husband] had been praying for
a break. We desperately needed to get away for a vacation,
but what God had in mind was much greater than we could
ever have dreamed.

"First of all, Graham won airline tickets as the
grand prize awarded last Christmas from our Chamber of
Commerce. Then we were offered a two week time-share
condominium, which the owner was not using, in Del Ray
Beach, Florida. Money came in, also, from a totally unex-
pected source for a car rental. So we were blessed with a
warm, beautiful Florida vacation in mid-winter. Can you
believe it?"

Yes, I could believe it. When God's people dare to
take steps of radical obedience, He is more than ready to
"open the windows of heaven and pour out a blessing we
cannot receive." You will note that this blessing came in
less than two months after they had destroyed the credit
cards.

Who among us is rich? Without question, it is he
who is content.

The grass may look greener on the other side of the
fence, but you can bet the water bill is higher. And I don't
want to pay it!

CHAPTER 12

A Different Drummer

Herein lies the glory of Christianity,
that God's treasure can be manifest
in every earthen vessel.[1]

Before I began jogging as a regular exercise routine, I was slightly critical of those "fresh-air idiots" who cluttered up the roadways by dashing alongside busy streets frustrating motorists. *Why don't they find some park or out-of-the-way place?* I'd mutter under my breath. Now that I have become addicted to this American mania, my attitude has changed drastically.

While in Seoul, South Korea, three years ago, I bought a jogging suit and running shoes which I carry with me all over the world. I arise early each morning and search out a scenic spot.

My jogging suit has witnessed magnificent sights. It has run beside the blue Mediterranean and the Sea of Galilee in Israel, on Waikiki Beach in Honolulu, in beautifully manicured parks in Tokyo, along fjords and breathtaking waterfalls in Norway, around the athletic field on the lovely grounds of the Foreign School in Seoul, all over a beautiful park in Guadalejara and one in Portsmouth, England—and certainly not least, the enticing wooded trails of the Roosevelt National Forest surrounding our home.

I have used that jogging suit so much that when it hangs in my closet, its contours automatically fall in the form of my body. And there's no question but that it knows how to jog. It has done so a million times.

But if I were to ask that suit to jump off the hanger and go jogging with me, it wouldn't budge. No matter what persuasive powers I might employ, my suit would never move. The reason is obvious, of course. Never once has it jogged without my body inside.

Ridiculous as this illustration sounds, it accurately represents the Christian life as God meant it to be lived. In the light of this metaphor, it would not be an exaggeration to say that *my life is simply that of Jesus, dressed up as Madalene.*

While that is a startling statement, nevertheless it is thoroughly scriptural. Every individual believer is merely a vehicle in which to carry the living, empowering Christ. This is what Paul meant when he said, ". . . your body is the temple of the Holy Spirit who is in you . . . and you are not your own . . ."[2] He also calls this principle a great mystery: ". . . Christ in you, the hope of glory."[3]

To become comfortable with this truth, try making the same statement by substituting your name in place of mine. Begin to picture yourself in that capacity. It will be awkward at first, but if you persist, you will begin to overcome a false idea of what the Christian life is all about.

If we ever fully comprehend this concept, we will no longer see ourselves as struggling pilgrims facing the crushing forces of evil alone. A new awareness of partnership will begin to surge through our imaginations to assure us we are "more than conquerors through Him that loved us."[4]

The Abiding Life

In fruit-growing states such as Oregon, my birthplace, the grafting of branches from one tree to another is as common as skiing in Colorado. My father often experimented with this process.

I remember a cherry tree in our yard that bore watery, tasteless fruit. We hated it and considered the bulky tree a waste. One summer my father grafted several branches from a Bing tree, and soon we had large quantities of luscious, black Bing cherries. The sustaining life of that large useless tree flowed through the fragile new branches enabling them to bear delicious fruit. Now we treasured the formerly worthless tree.

Our Lord Jesus uses branches and vines to describe the experience every true Christian is longing for. He calls that experience *abiding*. Instead of the jogging suit and the jogger, He envisions a vineyard full of branches and vines. Carefully read again the beloved passage:

> I am the true vine, and My Father is the vinedresser. Every branch in me that does not bear fruit, He takes away; and every branch that bears fruit, He prunes it that it may bear more fruit. You are already clean because of the word which I have spoken to you.
>
> Abide in Me, and I in you. As the branch cannot bear fruit of itself, unless it abides in the vine, so neither can you, unless you abide in Me.
>
> I am the vine, you are the branches; he who abides in Me, and I in him, he bears much fruit; for apart from Me, you can do nothing.[5]

So that we may fully understand what this abiding life means, a few symbolic terms need to be defined:

Vine . . . . Jesus.

Vinedresser . . God, the Father.

Branches . . . All believers.

Pruning . . . . . The vinedresser's method of producing fruit.

Fruit . . . . The fruit of the Spirit: ". . . love, joy, peace, longsuffering, gentleness, goodness, faith, meekness, and self-control."[6]

The Work of the Vinedresser

In this 20th century a vinedresser might be called a gardener or a nurseryman. His work is much the same as the biblical vinedresser. He makes all the decisions concerning the plants and trees, such as:

— Where to plant the vine.
— How much shade, sun, fertilizer, cultivation, etc.
— Condition of the soil.
— Season of planting.

Nothing is left to chance. For one whose livelihood depends upon the successful production of fruit, no decision is made haphazardly.

So if God is the heavenly Vinedresser, and every reborn child of His is represented as a branch on the vine, it might be well to ponder a few questions about the Vinedresser's choices in the planting of your life.

1. Is it possible you are living in the wrong location? Who decided to plant you there?

2. Could there be a mistake about your present circumstances? Who arranged them?

3. Are your current trials a matter of coincidence?

4. Is the Vinedresser (your heavenly Father) really in control — even when you don't realize it, or when you can't understand His reasoning?

Since the heavenly Vinedresser has decided all these matters, then why are you complaining? Why are you focusing all your strength toward changing these decisions so carefully made in your behalf?

The Function of the Vine

Thinking back on the illustration of the jogger in the suit, Jesus, the heavenly Vine, is like the jogger who provides all of the life and energy needed to transport the suit. His is the life-giving substance flowing through the branch to produce fruit. Without that substance, the branches wither and die.

What Is the Work of the Branch?

Most of us would answer immediately, "to bear fruit." It seems so obvious we don't need to consider anything else. But is that really our role?

In my childhood home state, Oregon, and on the western slope of Colorado, I have seen hundreds of orchards. In fact, we drive to Delta, Colorado every autumn to buy our winter supply of apples. Often we go out into an orchard and hand-pick them.

In all my experience, I have yet to see a branch on an apple tree appear worried about producing apples. Fruit occurs quite naturally as long as the branch remains connected to the tree.

We Christians often get sidetracked. Instead of pouring all our energies into staying firmly connected to the vine, we become detached by worrying about some particular aspect of our fruit-bearing.

"What's the matter with you?" I might ask the person who looks tense and defeated.

"Oh, I'm working on my witnessing. I just don't witness enough. I'm not bearing enough fruit."

This person is trying to do the work of the vine. When the life of the vine is flowing freely through the branch, beautiful blossoms grow without effort. And blossoms turn into fruit automatically.

The only prerequisite for a branch is to remain connected to that vine. Just abide. In no other way can we bear fruit. We may witness, teach and preach, and talk ourselves into oblivion, but unless we are abiding in the vine with the life of Christ flowing through us, no fruit will occur from all of these efforts.

Many believers have problems concerning Christ's statement: "If a branch abides not in me, He takes it away."[7] It is important to realize the He is not speaking about salvation here—only fruitbearing. So He is merely saying that if we continually fail to abide in Christ, we become detached and no fruit will grow. And sadly, that is the condition of many Christians today.

It is reported of Charles Haddon Spurgeon that it was not an uncommon sight to see him walking down a busy thoroughfare and suddenly stop, take off his hat, and bow his head for a few moments. Someone once asked what he was doing. He confided that when he became aware he was not abiding in Christ, wherever he was or whatever he was doing, he simply stopped to pray and make things right.

What About Pruning?

When my husband and I moved to North Carolina and our first pastorate, we had a huge house and a spacious yard. Many flowers already were planted and blooming, but since both of us were from Oregon, we couldn't feel right about not having fruit.

So we borrowed a pictorial seed catalog, looked at all the mouth-watering pictures, and finally decided to order grape vines. The description sounded fool-proof, even for beginners.

When our vines came, we couldn't believe what fell out of the package. Just a few scrawny, dead twigs. "Surely nothing will grow from these things," I said in disgust.

"We'll plant them anyway," my husband replied.

In no time at all those lifeless twigs began to grow and send shoots all over our fence. We remembered reading something in the planting directions about pruning, so we dug out the instructions to check.

After growth appears, prune plants to within three inches of ground, the instructions said.

"Three inches!" I shrieked. "That can't be right. Why, they'll never live."

"I don't remember my dad pruning back that much," my husband said.

We just couldn't do it. So together we decided simply to snip back a few inches and not cut off all the beautiful growth we were so proud of. Guess what happened? You're right. No fruit.

We learned our lesson the hard way. Next season we mercilessly pruned according to directions. You guessed it again. Fruit! Lots of it.

The same principle applies to us. No pruning, no fruit. Like the time-worn cliché, *No pain, no gain*. One does not happen without the other.

Pruning is for the sole purpose of producing fruit, not for the destruction of the vine or branch as my husband and I mistakenly thought. Without pruning, precious vitality for growth is siphoned off and strength to produce fruit is dissipated.

Even if we clearly see this principle in our gardening, it takes a great amount of spiritual maturity to recognize God's purposes for pruning in our lives. The reason is, pruning hurts. And none of us likes to hurt.

Even the instrument used for pruning attests to pain. It is sharp. I don't know if plants feel pain, but I do know pruning in the life of the believer is painful. I also know that if it didn't hurt, I, for one, would pay little attention.

It is important here to note what is cut off the tree in the process of pruning. In my understanding, the objects of pruning are three-fold and correspond to similar areas in our Christian lives.

First, dead branches are lopped off. These are fruitless, dead works. Nobody minds slashing branches from a tree that are obviously dead. Not only are they fruitless, but they detract from the overall beauty.

If we want to be fruit-bearers, God must remove those things from us that are either dead or promote spiritual death in us. These may include destructive habits, wrong friends or associates, worldly pursuits, sinful pleasures and the like. Living in the kind of seductively corrupt world surrounding us today, it is not difficult for Christians to become caught up in dead works.

Secondly, spurious shoots are removed. These are live, growing parts as contrasted to the dead branches. But they are growing in the wrong direction and do not contribute to the primary growth. In our lives, spurious shoots would be labeled as distractions.

The strange thing is that we are not always the best judges of what in our lives constitute distractions. Usually they are good things. Noble achievements.

This is not to say we shouldn't spend time doing good things. But if we crowd our days with wonderful activities that keep us from God's best and from His ultimate purpose for our existence, then we had better get serious about letting the Vinedresser remove what needs to be removed. "Let us throw off everything that hinders . . ."8

Most of us have a tendency to hang on to friendships, activities, and personal interests far longer than God can use them for fruitbearing in His vineyard. So He prunes them away, and in our ignorance we cry, "Why, Lord?"

Third, some good, healthy growth has to go. This aspect of pruning is the hardest to understand, both in the botanical world and in the spiritual. Beautiful, luxurious leaves and fruit surely can't be bad. Nevertheless, if the main stalk is threatened, nothing is worth sparing even good growth.

By now we have been stripped down to the bone. Dead works are gone, distractions and hindrances have been removed. So what is left for the Vinedresser's knife?

Ah, sad news that it is! Nothing is left but our good works, our cherished dreams, and our wonderful plans to serve the Lord.

"But Lord," we cry in our anguish, "this is for You. How could You think of destroying these noble plans I've made to serve You?"

What we can't understand is the reason why the Vinedresser must destroy these cherished dreams. Only in looking backwards do we ever get a glimpse into His eternal purposes.

For one thing, He knows that if I succeed greatly,

pride will enter. There is no limit to what God can do through any human being as long as that person doesn't care who gets the credit. But, you see, unless my plans and my purposes are pruned, I don't reach that point. Until then, it matters greatly that I get credit.

Personally, I believe this is the reason some of the greatly noted ministries of our day are crumbling. Too much pride, too much concern over visibility and credit. God won't put up with it.

Second, if my dreams are fulfilled before the who-gets-credit issue has been settled, I am tempted to regard the branch as more necessary than the vine. I therefore become detached and rendered fruitless.

In the early days of our ministry in North Carolina, my husband and I led a large Young Life Club. One of our boys who later became the southeast director of Young Life, Mal McSwain, prayed a prayer I have never forgotten. He was probably about seventeen when it happened.

"Lord," he said, "I just want to thank You for not giving me all the junk I've been asking You for."

That's how God views everything He is forced to prune from our lives—junk. And when it's gone, our vision clears and we are able to pray Mal McSwain's prayer.

The Shining Face

Two little verses from the Bible intrigue me. They are used in connection with Moses and Samson. They are:

"Moses wist not that the skin of his face shone."[9]

"Samson wist not that the Lord was departed."[10]

When Moses came down from Mount Sinai where He had seen the glory of the Lord during his forty-day conversation with Him, he didn't know that his face was shining. This gleaming countenance became such a terrifying distraction to his followers that they forced him to wear a veil.

A dear, little friend of ours, Lorri Scott, was recently saved. The best way I can describe her before Christ (B.C.)

is that she was thoroughly "hippy." She and her boyfriend, Mike, had been caught up in this appealingly carefree lifestyle and headed out in their beat-up station wagon from New York to travel whichever way the wind blew.

The wind blew to Colorado Springs where the Lord had a big surprise awaiting Lorri and Mike. Both of them were gloriously saved and became immediately convicted that God didn't want them living together. Eventually Lorri landed a job at one of the many Christian organizations based in Colorado Springs.

She loved her work, her new surroundings, and all the Christians she became associated with. But one day she told me, "You know, Madalene, the people I work with are wonderful. They are such mature Christians. They know the Bible backwards and forwards, and I sometimes envy that knowledge."

Then she paused, as if in deep thought. "But something is wrong. I just can't put my finger on it."

After a little more pondering, she hit the problem squarely. "I know what it is!" she exclaimed. "There's no shine on their faces. That's it. Do you understand what I mean?"

Out of the mouth of babes, I thought. This infant Christian had the mature judgment to identify a pathetic deficiency common to many long-time believers. No wonder so few are attracted to the beauty and loveliness of the Lord Jesus. All they see on our faces are furrowed brows, anxious expressions, and evidence of feverish pace. No time to reach out and touch each other.

How do we lose our shine? It happens so gradually we hardly perceive it. Whenever we revert to fleshly ability to accomplish the work of God, this subtle erosion begins eating away. Soon we become disconnected from our Source of life and energy, and we fail to detect it.

We become like Samson, who didn't even know that the presence of the Lord had left him. He was God's chosen man, separated from the moment of his birth to do a great work for God's kingdom. But he failed because he didn't learn to depend upon God's strength rather than his own.

How quickly we forget that we are only the branches, and not the vine. We get so busily occupied trying to accomplish the work of the vine that we fail to remain dependently attached to our source.

Back to the "Shine"

It's easy to spot those Christians with shining faces who have climbed God's mountain. They are the ones who move happily through life with unruffled spirits. Interruptions rarely perturb them, catastrophes only strengthen them, criticism doesn't antagonize them, and they always have time to lift up a faltering brother or sister.

The reason so few of us ever manage to climb the heights and partake of God's glory is because our efforts remain stagnated in mere wishful thinking. We look up and see the majesty on top. We long for the peace. We ardently desire to breathe the pure air. But we don't seem to get moving. Or if we do, we begin sliding backwards before making significant progress. Although we are busily engaged with our indispensable labor in God's kingdom, we never lift our eyes to behold our glorious King.

But we do have a choice. We can stay in the stifling flatlands of daily monotony, spiritual dullness, and unexciting routine—or we can face those crippling barriers, overcome them with God's grace, and move upward to the most exciting adventure life offers.

Don't waste another day. Start heading up that glorious mountain!

Madalene Harris is available to speak at conferences and retreats. For more information, please write:

>Madalene Harris
>c/o Here's Life Publishers
>P. O. Box 1576
>San Bernardino, CA 92402-1576

Notes

Chapter 1

1. Elisabeth Elliott, *The Journals of Jim Elliott* (Old Tappan, NJ: Fleming H. Revell Company, 1978), p. 275.

2. Dr. James Davis, associate professor of psychology at Southwest Missouri State University, Springfield, MO. (Visiting professor in sports psychology, United States Olympic Center, Colorado Springs, 1986.)

3. Luke 9:57 (NIV).

4. Luke 9:58 (NIV).

5. Luke 9:59 (NIV).

6. Archibald D. Hart, *Adrenalin and Stress* (Waco, TX: Word Books, 1986), p. 46.

7. Luke 10:42 (NIV).

8. Oswald J. Chambers, *My Utmost for His Highest* (New York: Dodd, Mead, and Company, 1935), p. 195.

9. Lloyd J. Ogilvie, *If God Cares, Why Do I Still Have Problems?* (Waco, TX: Word Books, 1985), p. 92.

10. Philippians 4:13.

11. 2 Corinthians 5:17.

12. James 1:5.

13. Paul Lee Tan, *Encyclopedia of 7,700 Illustrations* (Maryland: Assurance Publishers, 1979).

Chapter 2

1. Oswald Chambers, *My Utmost for His Highest,* p. 318.

2. Paraphrased from *Telling Yourself the Truth* by William Backus and Marie Chapian (Minneapolis, MN: Bethany Fellowship, Inc., 1980), p. 8.

3. Cecil Osborne, *The Art of Understanding Yourself* (Grand Rapids, MI: Zondervan Publishing Company, 1967), p. 37.

4. Backus and Chapian, *Telling Yourself the Truth,* p 71.

5. Matthew 11:28 (NIV).

6. Hebrews 4:10,11.

7. Philippians 4:19.

8. Ephesians 3:20.

9. Philippians 4:13 (NIV).

10. James 4:7 (NIV).

11. Tan, *Encyclopedia of 7,700 Illustrations.*

Chapter 3

1. Carole Mayhall, *Words That Hurt, Words That Heal* (Colorado

Springs, CO: NavPress, 1986), p. 38.

2. Philippians 2:14 (NIV).
3. 1 Thessalonians 5:18 (KJV).
4. Romans 8:28 (KJV).
5. Jess Stein, ed., *The Random House College Dictionary* (New York: Random House, Inc., 1980).
6. Mayhall, *Words That Hurt, Words That Heal,* p. 41.

Chapter 4

1. Gary Collins, *The Magnificent Mind* (Waco, TX: Word Publishing Co., 1985), p. 78.
2. Jerry Garlitz, Colorado Springs counselor and Naval Reserve clinical psychologist.
3. Ephesians 4:32 (NASB).
4. Catherine Jackson, *The Christian's Secret of a Happy Life for Today,* A Paraphrase of Hannah Whitall Smith's Classic (Old Tappan, NJ: Fleming H. Revell Company, 1979), p. 76.
5. Leviticus 24:20 (NIV).
6. Matthew 5:38-41.
7. Matthew 18:21.
8. Matthew 6:15 (NIV).

Chapter 5

1. Elisabeth Elliott, *Obedience, The Glad Surrender* (Old Tappan, NJ: Fleming H. Revell Company, 1982), p. 37.
2. *The Random House College Dictionary,* Revised Edition, 1980.
3. C. S. Lewis, *Sexual Morality,* Book Three.
4. Luke 6:46 (NIV).
5. James 2:26.
6. 1 Corinthians 6:20.
7. Romans 13:1,2 (NIV).
8. Chambers, *My Utmost For His Highest,* p. 284.

Chapter 6

1. John G. Mitchell, *An Everlasting Love* (Portland, OR: Multnomah Press, 1982), p. 168.
2. John 16:33.
3. John 6:35.
4. John 15:3.
5. James 1:23.
6. Ephesians 4:29 (NIV).
7. Psalm 119:105 (NIV).
8. The *Topical Memory System* is published by NavPress and is available at your local Christian bookstore.

Chapter 7

1. Chambers, *My Utmost for His Highest.*
2. 2 Corinthians 10:4.
3. John 14:13,14.
4. Philippians 4:19.
5. Chambers, *My Utmost for His Highest*, p. 147.
6. Bill Bright, *How to Pray*, A Transferable Concept (San Bernardino, CA: Here's Life Publishers, 1971).
7. Chambers, *My Utmost for His Highest*, p. 236.
8. Ibid, p. 29.
9. James 1:6,7 (NIV).
10. Timothy 2:2.

Chapter 8

1. David C. Needham, *Birthright* (Portland, OR: Multnomah Press, 1979), p. 60.
2. Romans 8:17.
3. 2 Corinthians 5:17.
4. Romans 6:13.
5. Romans 8:37.
6. Philippians 4:13.
7. Philippians 4:19.
8. Ephesians 1:5 (NIV).
9. Galatians 4:5.
10. 1 Corinthians 2:12.
11. 2 Corinthians 5:17 (NIV).
12. Needham, *Birthright*, p. 123.
13. Philippians 4:13.
14. Matthew 19:26.
15. Genesis 18:14.

Chapter 9

1. Chambers, *My Utmost for His Highest.*
2. Richard J. Foster, *Freedom of Simplicity* (San Francisco, CA: Harper & Row Publishers, 1981), p. 95.
3. Matthew 26:33 (NIV).
4. John 16:24.
5. Philippians 1:21.
6. Philippians 4:13.
7. Philippians 3:10.
8. Matthew 18:3,4 (NIV).

Chapter 10

1. Chambers, *My Utmost for His Highest*, p. 102.
2. Psalm 19:14 (NIV).
3. Romans 7:18b (NIV).

4. Matthew 7:11 (NIV).
5. Jackson, *The Christian's Secret of a Happy Life for Today,* p. 124.
6. Chambers, *My Utmost for His Highest,* p. 333.
7. Galatians 3:3 (NASB).
8. From a sermon by evangelist Jack Taylor.
9. Ibid.
10. Acts 8:19.
11. Chambers, *My Utmost For His Highest,* p. 244.
12. Galatians 2:20 (NASB).
13. Acts 1:8.
14. Philippians 3:8.
15. Hebrews 12:1 (NASB).
16. Psalm 51:4 (NIV).
17. Watchman Nee, *Twelve Baskets Full,* Vol. 2 (New York: Christian Literature Crusade, 1972), p. 146.
18. Ibid. p. 147.
19. Romans 12:1.
20. Tan, *Encyclopedia of 7700 Illustrations.*
21. Luke 11:13 (NIV).

Chapter 11

1. Tan, *Encyclopedia of 7,700 Illustrations.*
2. Foster, *Freedom of Simplicity,* p. 3.
3. Osgood, Don, *Pressure Points* (New York: Christian Herald Books, 1978), p. 111.
4. Hebrews 13:5.
5. Philippians 4:11.
6. Philippians 4:4 (TLB).
7. Tan, *Encyclopedia of 7,700 Illustrations.*
8. 1 Thessalonians 5:18.
9. Philippians 3:10.
10. Elliott, *Discipline, The Glad Surrender,* p. 109.
11. Philippians 1:29 and 2 Timothy 2:12.
12. Foster, *Freedom of Simplicity,* p. 120.

Chapter 12

1. Nee, *Twelve Baskets Full,* Vol.2. p. 30.
2. 1 Corinthians 6:19 (NASB).
3. Colossians 1:27.
4. Romans 8:37.
5. John 15:1-6 (NASB).
6. Galatians 5:22,23.
7. John 15:3.
8. Hebrews 12:1 (NIV).
9. Exodus 34:29.
10. Judges 16:20.